SWEET ODYSSEY

IDARIO SANTOS

Sweet Odyssey – A Must Read True Story
Forward by Kevin A. Strauss, M.D.

The legend of King Arthur is one of courage, valor, and loyalty; it is a story of heroic actions in the face of extraordinary odds. *Sweet Odyssey* tells a similar tale, but with one important exception. *It is true*. Its main protagonists, young "King" Artur Santos and his father Idario, are real-life heroes; made of flesh and blood. In *Sweet Odyssey*, you will learn that the challenges faced by the mythical King Arthur pale in comparison to those overcome by one courageous young boy and his family. *Sweet Odyssey* will teach you how real heroes think and act, drawing on deep reserves of integrity, resourcefulness, and perseverance in the face of almost unimaginable obstacles. Perhaps more importantly, *Sweet Odyssey* will teach you something about love; all who read the story of young Artur and his remarkable family will come away with a deeper understanding of the love that binds us to one another, and the sacrifices it entails. In my work as a physician, I am sometimes moved deeply by the sacrifices parents make on behalf of their children, and often by the selfless courage of the children themselves. These children teach us something different, more penetrating, than all the facts we can glean from medical textbooks. They teach us the true meaning of *compassion*.

Kevin A. Strauss, M.D.
Strasburg, March 2014

Short Biography

Kevin A. Strauss, who earned his M.D. from Harvard Medical School, is medical director of the Clinic for Special Children in Strasburg, Pa.
Some Important scientific journals published by Dr. Kevin Strauss
Prevention of Brain Disease from Severe 5,10-methylenetetrahydrofolate Reductase Deficiency. Kevin A. Strauss et al. in Molecular Genetics and Metabolism, Vol. 91, No. 2, pages 165–175; June 2007.

Genetics, Medicine, and the Plain People. Kevin A. Strauss and Erik G. Puffenberger in Annual Review of Genomics and Human Genetics, Vol. 10, pages 513–536; September 2009.

One Community's Effort to Control Genetic Disease. Kevin A. Strauss, Erik G. Puffenberger and D. Holmes Morton in American Journal of Public Health, Vol. 102, No. 7, pages 1300–1306; July 2012.

A Population-Based Study of KCNH7 p.Arg394His and Bipolar Spectrum Disorder. Kevin A. Strauss et al. in Human Molecular Genetics, Vol. 23, No. 23, pages 6395–6406; December 1, 2014.

Sweet Odyssey

The importance of Newborn Screening

Early diagnosis of any genetic disease has the potential to prevent severe health problems, including the most extreme condition, death. Newborn screening has evolved to the point that over 50 different genetic conditions can be detected. However, only a few countries have implemented a comprehensive testing program and the number of tests done on a routine basis can vary within those countries, depending on state requirements. For example, according to "Empresa Brasileira de Cominicação - EBC", in Brazil, more than 13,000,000 people suffer from some type of genetic disorder, like my brother. There, the number of screening tests also varies from state to state, with an average of only 4 genetic disorders being tested. In some other countries, this type of testing does not even occur. Newborns from around the world are lacking a proper newborn screening. The neglected children suffering from genetic disorders need your help. **Let's give them a chance**. "Sweet Odyssey" will teach you how.

VINICIUS SANTOS
Co-Author

FOREWORD

Odyssey is a classic poem credited to Homer, describing Odysseus's adventures in his ten-year attempt to return home after the Trojan War. An "odyssey" by characterization is a long meandering trip or journey usually marked by many changes of luck!

In April 2014, I was invited to speak at a public hearing - the Programa Seminario Triagem Neonatal - held in Sao Paulo, Brazil on May 19-23, 2014. My assigned task was to discuss the process of how the screening test panel (Recommended Universal Screening Panel, RUSP) was originated in the US and how future disorders are added to this panel. At that time, Brazil did not have a national newborn screening program with population-based screening for an established uniform screening panel of disorders. At this meeting, I was introduced for the first time to Idario Santos (a Brazilian parent). During the coffee breaks, Idario and I spoke about his traumatic experiences with his second son who was eventually diagnosed with a metabolic disorder outside of a newborn screening program. After the meeting, he presented me with an autographed copy of his book, *"Uma Doce Odisseia."* It was in Portuguese, and I could not even comprehend the title. Idario and I developed a friendship during our discussions. Impressed with his story, I arranged for him to present it to the US newborn screening community during the 2014 National Newborn Screening Symposium held in Anaheim, CA. His presentation was well received by the participants.

The book, "Sweet Odyssey," is a life-based, true account of a Brazilian man, Idario Santos, who finds himself for over a decade in positions comparable to those of the Biblical character, Job. Most everyone has heard of the suffering of Job in the Bible's Old Testament. Before January 2002, a couple weeks after all the excitement from the birth of his second son, Artur, Idario was extremely happy and all seemed well in his world. He was becoming well-situated financially, had a happy family and a good business in his home city of Petrolina, Brazil. Idario had no idea how his life was headed toward a dreadful existence of radical change with continuous daily trials and tribulations. Future events and struggles were going to prove how little control that he had over life's challenges or how strong his religious faith and emotional strength were. These strengths would transform him into a man on an obsessed mission to conquer a multiplicity of barriers and challenges placed before him by odd circumstances and difficult people in places of authority.

His son began to develop medical problems a few weeks after birth and the diagnostic odyssey—the persistent search for an explanation of a health problem—was underway to first identify the cause of the problem and then to find a treatment. After a few months and numerous hospital visits, internet searching, and encounters with physicians, little Artur was diagnosed with a metabolic disorder called Maple Syrup Urine Disorder (MSUD). This began the second phase of Idario's mission to find treatment and ideally a cure while worrying about the current developing outcomes for his son during this progression. Idario had help from his families and made many new friends during his journey. The internet became his tool for seeking help and learning about the disorder that eventually lead to his chance encounter with Dr. Kevin Strauss , the world expert on MSUD. While traveling this odyssey, Idario lost all his property, wealth, job, and became deeply indebted to many people, but he never wavered from his mission or faith. His wife, first son and family stood by Idario through all the difficulties, numerous relocations and the endeavors with Drs. Holmes Morton and Kevin Strauss at the Clinic for Special Children in Lancaster, PA and with the medical staff at the transplantation center of the Pittsburgh Children's Hospital. The family unit, although stretched by the odyssey, remained intact and stronger. Idario proved that he is truly a very tenacious man who achieved his life-time desire to emulate the tenacity of his father.

The story is an adventure filled with heart-break after heart-break and occasionally joy. The described struggles and challenges were in most cases tearful and sad. The book is a first-rate read, embracing all the elements of life's experiences, including the one that frequently does not occur, a happy ending. It is amazing that the author had the ability to retain and express all the traumas that he had faced; the intense struggles, the harsh treatments by physicians, the indifferent government officials, and the loss of all of his material possessions. I found it captivating how much a father was willing to sacrifice and the suffering he could place on his family and his first son, all for the health quest of his second son. In my career, I have heard of numerous odysseys associated with newborn screening outcomes and failures--most of which are terrible and have sad outcomes. "Sweet Odyssey" has many terrible and sad events, unbelievable challenges, but all real life happenings for someone somewhere and it ends with happiness for all. The reader learns that life's struggles require an enormous amount of faith and perseverance to perhaps achieve success -- no guarantee, but certainly one gains greater strength for future challenges. I strongly recommend this book to all parents, grandparents, newborn screeners, and healthcare professionals as a must read!!

By: William Harry Hannon, PhD
Independent Consultant and Retired Chief, Newborn Screening Branch and Founder, Newborn Screening Quality Assurance Program (NSQAP) Centers for Disease Control and Prevention (CDC)
November 2015

Short Biography

Dr. Hannon retired from the Centers for Disease Control and Prevention (CDC) with 41 years of service. He was Chief of the CDC's Newborn Screening Branch for over 25 years and retired as the Acting Branch Chief of the recently organized Newborn Screening and Molecular Biology Branch. In 1978, he created the Newborn Screening Quality Assurance Program at the CDC, which provides services to all U.S. newborn screening laboratories and to over 400 laboratories in 54 countries. He has over 250 scientific publications and has served on over 30 national and international committees for a variety of laboratory issues. Dr. Hannon co-authored standards for WHO for designing and implementing congenital hypothyroid and PKU neonatal screening in developing and developed countries. He has received many awards for his scientific contributions, including the

Robert Guthrie Award in 1999, two CDC Shepard Awards [CDC's preeminent science award] - 1992 and 2005, the 2006 Walter Dowdle Award, the 2008 Association of Public Health Laboratories (APHL)'s Lifetime Achievement Award, and the Clinical and Laboratory Standards Institute's (CLSI), Russell J. Eilers Memorial Award 2008 [the highest CLSI honor award]. APHL created the Harry Hannon Laboratory Improvement Award in Newborn Screening, which was awarded for the first time in 2008. In 2009, he received the Jeffrey Modell Foundation's "Dream Makers" Award in New York City for his contributions to early detection of primary immune deficiency disorders by newborn screening. Since retirement, Dr. Hannon has continued his work to initiate, expand and improve newborn screening worldwide.

THIS BOOK IS DEDICATED TO:

THE MEN IN MY LIFE

Grandpa Sebastian - You were full of grace. I wish you could have read this book, but we always understood each other and I know that printed words will never change our feelings toward one another. God is with you, as He has always been.

Dear Dad – You are a great man and have always taken such good care of us all. Your principles of dignity, tenacity and honesty will certainly be an inspiration through generation after generation of the Santos family.

Dear Vini - Five years ago when I began to write this book, you were a kid and now you've become a mature and responsible young man. You remind me so much of your Mom's brother, Arquimedes. If you follow his example, I am certain that you will be a great man.

Make sure you read this book and then keep it close at hand, so that when you are looking for some inner peace, you can just pick it up and read it again. Then, you'll be reminded of your roots. Perhaps I won't be physically beside you, but I'll always be with you in spirit.

Dear Artur – You are the strongest person that I have ever known. You are my life's teacher. I really see Jesus in you. Even in your most difficult times, you always smiled, seeming to try to comfort me. Your happiness shined through even when sadness surrounded you. Your limitless love inspired us. Thank you so very much.

MY TWO LOVABLE LADIES:

Mom – Perhaps, when Grandpa Nogueira chose your name, Beatriz (Beatrice in English), he didn't know what it meant and I guess you never knew, but Beatrice means BLESSED. You are blessed in truth. You bless everyone with your great charisma. You are an amazing peacemaker.

Soraya – My adorable wife, what would my life be without you? I thank our Lord for bringing us together. You have a great heart and you are a fountain of inspiration to every woman on earth. I love you so very much.

ALL OF YOU

Dear all – Please take this true story as a lesson, understanding that everything in life has a purpose. You just need to understand God's desires and you'll be blessed.

Contents:

INTRODUCTION

Undoubtedly, life is like a huge 'chest' with unknown contents. Each day, we reach inside and never know what's coming out. This book tells the story of a complex, fateful odyssey, a fighting king's spirit, and a family's struggle to save a child's threatened life, all while living in a new and unfamiliar country.

Along the way, some people come to realize the importance of having a global view as they face life's challenges and to form a personal opinion about the spiritual presence of God.

Given the environment in which we live, it seems that most people set their goals and then struggle to achieve them, while focusing constantly on increasing their personal wealth. Happiness will be assured if only they acquire certain dreams, such as buying a brand new car, living in a huge house, having a chance of enjoying those dreamed vacations, etc. In short, possessing "things and or living some moments" will eventually lead them to happiness. But as they reach for that dream from the life's huge 'chest', sometimes they pull out a nightmare.

I agree that people need their dreams and should pursue them. After all, we human beings must have resources to survive and to achieve our goals. However, no goal is worth sacrificing one's integrity.

In pursuit of happiness, people often look for shortcuts. They never think about the obstacles they may face along the way. These obstacles may force them to detour, delay or even abandon their plans. A family member's affliction with a rare disease will certainly become an obstacle in life's path that can force a family in another direction. Facing such an obstacle, people really don't know where they are headed or where they will end up. Such is the detour that my family and I were forced to follow.

These detours can lead us to a feeling of complete helplessness as we try to find the right path. Dealing with rare diseases is also compounded when even medical professionals are at a loss on how to deal with the situation. On this detour, we also encounter all kinds of people. Some will push us to give up and go another way; some will summon God and suggest that we leave it in his hands; some will be totally wrong and others very helpful. In a very tough situation, being wise is extremely important. Our emotions can easily lead us to failure especially when we have skeptical people surrounding us.

Maybe I still do not know what happiness is. The detour I was forced to take as I describe in this book has become my destiny, and I believe this is my road to achieving happiness. Who knows what I will pull next from the life's huge 'chest', but I thank God every day for what has happened in my life so far.

Idario Santos

2016

CHAPTER 1

A PARALYZED LIFE

Dark are the days when all of our hopes inexplicably dissolve, followed by events that complicate life in unimaginable ways

"*Your son is in a coma!*" It was two weeks after the birth of my second son, Artur, when his doctor pierced my soul with this statement. Now, when I think about that day in January 2002, I realize that my life had forever changed. Time seemed to pass in slow motion and I was living in an eternity of doubts, exams, inaccurate diagnoses, hospitals, and needles.

Yes, my two-week old son was in a coma, living like a vegetable. He couldn't open his eyes. The veins in his arms were about to collapse from all the blood tests. Sometimes, nurses even had to take samples from his head. The doctors were bewildered. They had no idea what was affecting our baby or what to do to help him. Only my wife, Soraya, and I had permission to enter into the ICU. Our cell phones never stopped ringing. Relatives and friends were calling every minute, but we had no news for them. Our callers only knew that our anxiety level was high.

Thirty days later we finally had a diagnosis, Leukodystrophy. When I hung up a phone call from my mother-in-law, I left my parents' house almost to the point of weeping. I felt like the world was crumbling around me. Why was this happening to me? Why is this happening to my son? What had I done wrong to be punished in such way? My wife must have been horrified. To me, she had already suffered enough! I felt like the most insignificant person in the world. To me, it seemed to be the end, and in my desperation, I proposed a pact to God: "*Lord, why are you doing this to me? If it's Your will, take my life for the happiness of my wife and my children. From now on, You do what You want with me, but please protect my family.*"

Throughout the day, doctors were throwing around names of diseases that fall into the category of Leukodystrophy, like Phenylketonuria, Urea Cycle disorder and MSUD. And one of them caught my attention: MSUD, that is, Maple Syrup Urine Disease. I had been doing some online research when it hit me. The symptoms of this disease were very similar to the way Artur was right after he was born.

Could this possibly be my son's mystery disease?

That night, I was with Artur in the ICU while my wife was praying in a small hospital chapel. Knowing her, she would be asking for our son and for our family's happiness. I looked at him in his incubator, imagining that we needed a true miracle to save him.

Then, the unexpected happened. My little boy moved his left arm. Were our prayers being answered? I turned around to see if anyone else had seen this, but God, his many angels and I were the only ones there. This time, I knew it from the bottom of my heart that it was not a fantasy that I had created out of despair. Seeing Artur as a fighter that would never give up, I declared to myself that he was not only my boy, but my little king, like the legendary King Arthur.

With Artur coming out of his coma, our hope grew, and my desire to fight gave me a new persona. From that day on, I would be a knight for my King Artur. In his stead, I would fight all battles to find the Grail that would save his life. Like the Arthurian legends, only the Grail would return peace to the kingdom. Only Artur's cure, my Grail, would give us peace. Beside me, I had my lady, Soraya, and my fellow knave, Vinicius. Without them, I would have succumbed to the pain of the journey and given in.

At this moment, all of us had merged into a cross-cultural life of struggle, unfulfilled promises, pain and happiness, mazes, faith and hope. A new life so different from the one that we had known or planned had just begun.

CHAPTER 2

THE GENESIS

My grandfather extolled his own son,
And I imagined myself to be like my own father, a tenacious man

I left Prata, my birthplace, when I was a baby, so I have always considered Petrolina my hometown. This amazing city is located at the southernmost point in the Brazilian state of Pernambuco along the São Francisco River. This scenic river divides Petrolina from its twin city of Juazeiro in the state of Bahia. An agro-industrial city, Petrolina is the home of hard-working families and little else. But Juazeiro is quite the opposite - a city of festivals, good restaurants, nightclubs, and a fabulous carnival. People from Petrolina like to say that they make money in Petrolina and spend it in Juazeiro. I think it's true. As a kid, I spent a lot of time enjoying the attractions in Juazeiro.

It was along the São Francisco River that my brothers and I had our biggest adventures. Besides fishing and swimming, it was there that we used to gather with other kids and play soccer for hours and then cool off in the river. My oldest brother was the most courageous boy in our gang. Very often, he scared me to death when he jumped off a bridge. It was prohibited, but he didn't give a damn about the law. I could sense when he was going to do something crazy, and when I would shout, "Please don't go! Dad will be mad at you and the police can arrest you!"

"Don't be a baby! The cops won't come here. And, if they do, they can't catch me."

"Please don't do it."

"Shut up. I'll be back in a little bit. Today, I am going to do the 'pencil jump' and don't even dare to tell Dad. You know what happens to you if you tell him, don't you?"

He was strong and I would never tell my parents about his crazy adventures. I was just afraid of losing my brother. We had already witnessed some drowning deaths in this river.

Compared to my brothers, I was the only one who had a very good childhood. As the youngest, I always felt safe. My brothers wouldn't let anybody touch me and I pretty much could do whatever I wanted. In my early teens, I remember that my brothers' and sisters' lives were not very easy. Everyone but me was working to help our parents make ends meet. I guess someone could say that I was spoiled. I was the only one studying at a private Catholic school and I had no responsibilities at home.

In my teens, I loved going to my grandpa's house to eat supper and listen to his amazing stories. Some of Grandpa Sebastião's stories were purely from his imagination. But as a storyteller, nobody could beat him. He had a way of delivering a story that would often make us laugh. Whether true or imagined, however, his stories always taught us something good.

One of the stories that I loved the most was about the beginning of our family. Grandpa would start by saying that my dad was a tenacious person and he knew that my father, Hilário, would make his dreams come true. Back in the 50's, when he was in his late teens, my dad would come to grandpa once in a while saying: 'Dad, one day, I'll have my own land, and I'll have my own crops.'

Grandpa went on, "But, opportunities were limited, especially in this area of Brazil, which, even today, is still the one of the poorest regions in the country. Despite the tough times, Hilário and your mother, Beatriz, married and soon had twins. Unfortunately, the babies died within a few months of birth; the cause was never determined."

Knowing the history of my family taught me a lot and helped me especially when I needed to face many obstacles, so I always was attentive.

Grandpa continued, "In time, Hilário started his own farm, achieving one of his dreams. By then, two girls, Ildenice and Irenice, had been born and your Mom was pregnant with Isnaldo. At this time, a prolonged drought forced him to abandon his farming activity. He came to me saying,

'Dad, I am broke! I am going to São Paulo. This is no longer a place where I can support my family.'

'But what are you going to do in São Paulo?'

'I don't know. I'll find a job and I'll do my best to support my family. We can't live forever in poverty and waiting for God to bring rain to this dry land.'

"It was 1963, when my only son was totally broke and headed to São Paulo, the fastest growing Brazilian city at the time. It took him seventeen days to get there in the back of a truck known as 'Pau de Arara.'"

One of us would interrupt him. "Grandpa, what is a Pau de Arara?"

"Literally translated, it is a macaw's perch, but for our Northeastern people, this is a designation given to a flat-bed truck adapted for passenger transportation. The truck's bed is equipped with narrow wooden benches and a canvas canopy. I can tell you that this kind of transport was very slow and very uncomfortable. And back then, it was the common way to travel between cities. But, when Hilário reached São Paulo, he soon found jobs. He worked as a clerk in a bakery in the mornings and peddled merchandise on the streets in the afternoons for two long years. After two years, your mom came to my house showing me a letter."

She said, "Look, my father-in-law, this is a letter from your son. He is on his way back. He says here that he is bringing some money and we'll start a new business. He has good plans for all of us."

"In 1965, as soon as your dad returned to our hometown of Prata, Hilário opened a gambling house, a legal enterprise at the time. I, along with others, walked house-to-house selling tickets for his 'animal game'(similar to state lottery games in the United States). At first, this gaming business supported our families very well. After couple of years, though, gambling became illegal in Brazil and he was forced to abandon it. Still today, I remember when he came to me in tears.

"He said, 'Dad, we are broke again. I don't know what to do…'

"With no option, Hilário went back to work as a farm laborer. By now, Beatriz had had two more babies, Ivaldo and Ildeci."

"In 1968, your mom's father, Mr. Nogueira, inherited a little hotel and restaurant here in Petrolina. Your maternal grandfather came to Petrolina to check out this business, but didn't like the idea of leaving his hometown. So, he offered this business to Hilário, telling him that this could be a fresh start for him. Hilário agreed and immediately accepted his father-in-law's offer. However, before packing up the family for Petrolina, there was an unplanned addition to the family."

Pointing his finger to me, grandpa continued:

"Yes, you! If I am not mistaken, you were born in December 1968, right before your family departure to Petrolina.

"But, let me tell you. The restaurant was a nightmare. It had no doors and was opened 24 hours, 7 days a week. Your parents had no rest. Years later, Hilário sold the business in good faith to a buyer whose unscrupulous negotiations led to a bad deal. The business was gone without much to show for it. And guess what? Hilário was broke again. He went to talk to Mr. Antonio Queiroz, a very successful owner of several retail businesses in town. He was a customer at the restaurant. Hilário asked if he could work as a salesman in one of his stores. Instead, Mr. Queiroz offered him work as a street peddler. Hilário decided to give it a try and put his feet to the pavement.

"After months as a peddler, I went to visit him in Petrolina. He then told me, 'Dad, you can come and live with us here in Petrolina. I found a place in a public market. I can have my own store and you can work with me.'

"I accepted his offer because years of drought had again ravaged our region. So, for some years, I worked with Hilário in his new and promising business."

When grandpa mentioned this part, I could picture this scene. At this time, I was about seven years old, and still today, I can recall grandpa's, my dad's and brothers' routine, hauling miscellaneous merchandise in wheelbarrows to sell them in an improvised tent in Petrolina's public market. I still remember that every day. Dad came home very tired, but I remember that he still had plenty of time for me.

Grandpa then continued his story, "Throughout these difficult times, your mother, a strong partner with Hilário, was caring for her large family. On her own, she started sewing for neighbors and made decorative blankets to sell from home. Her business prospered, so, along with Hilário's growing success, they decided to open their own store in downtown Petrolina. After years of struggling, this business, called 'Armarinho Cruz de Prata,' became the solid foundation for our family."

I loved when grandpa extolled his own son, and I imagined myself being just like my dad, a tenacious man that never gives up.

CHAPTER 3

LOVE AND YOUTH

Listen to your heart when it's calling for you.

Throughout Brazil, universities administer an annual test called 'Vestibular.' The Vestibular (from Portuguese: *vestíbulo*, 'entrance hall') is a competitive examination used by Brazilian universities to evaluate prospective students. The vestibular usually takes place from November to January, right before the start of the school year in February or March. The exams often span several days with different disciplines being tested each day. This was a great time for university veterans to scout out the incoming freshmen girls. After the exams, the atmosphere became like our annual Carnival.

In 1990, I decided to stay in town and enjoy the vestibular festivities. On a Saturday night, my buddy, Joelio, and I went to the most bustling dance bar. We ordered a couple of beers and saw a friend, Lela, who invited us to join her and her two very good-looking girlfriends. Lela introduced us to the 'vestibulandas' (a name used for girls who are taking the vestibular test). Joelio and I went to get another beer and, out of earshot from the girls, I said, "I am taking the one with the short hair. I guess her name is Zoraide."

"But, she is not even looking at you and she doesn't seem to be in the mood," he said

"Don't worry; I'll take care of her."

"All right, I am fine in taking the other one. And I am sure that her name is Delma. She has a good body. Did you see when she went to the bathroom?" he said.

"Yes I did. She looks good."

Back with the girls, I was on my second beer, when out of the blue, I knocked my hand on the table and pointed my finger at her and shouted:

"Zoraide, no matter what, today, I am going to kiss you."

I don't really know what came over me; this was totally out of my character. At this point, I figured that I had blown my chances with this girl. I thought to myself. "*What am I doing?*" Almost instantaneously, she angrily replied:

"What is your problem? You don't even know me!"

Despite being devastated on the inside, I was compelled to keep up the facade.

"Well, we'll see. You'll like us. Besides, we are the only people who can show you guys the good places here in town."

Due to my arrogance, I was about to lose my chance with this girl. Even though I regretted my initial approach, I did not lose confidence. Leaving the bar, we all went to a nightclub. There, I invited Zoraide to dance and right then, I could show my talent. After dancing the 'forró', a typical Brazilian dance step, the DJ luckily started playing one of Roxette's songs, 'Listen to Your Heart.' She wanted to quit dancing, but I begged for one more. She accepted and I started apologizing:

"I am sorry for the way that I started our conversation. I hope you don't get the wrong impression of me!"

"Truly, I didn't like your attitude. You embarrassed me. But that's OK, apology accepted," she said

"But, even though I was a little snobbish, I meant every word. I still want to kiss you."

"You said a LITTLE snobbish? If this is a little, I can't imagine when you get totally snobbish."

"Yeah. But, I am not like that. Just give me a chance and you'll see."

"Let's go back to our table and we'll talk about this later…"

In the end, after more dancing, a couple more beers, and good conversation, my persuasion worked out and by midnight I was kissing my girl. She spent a few more days in Araripina and then she went back to her city of Fortaleza.

Not long after our meeting, I heard that Zoraide had passed the test and in two months, I would see her again. But, when she came to live near my house, which I shared with four other students and named it 'Republica dos Bananas', things started changing in my life.

After dating her for about one week, I only then realized that her name was not Zoraide, as I had been thinking all along, but Soraya.

In a few months, Soraya and I were in love and a new generation of Santoses was started.

CHAPTER 4

A NEW GENERATION

Hopeful are the days where you're waiting for something that will bring joy

Soraya was very supportive, always encouraging me to complete my degree, despite my ongoing willingness to abandon college and return to my life as a farmer. Three months before graduation, I moved to Mauriti in northeast Brazil to work as an agricultural engineer. There, I used my skills to design and install mango and banana orchards for a 450-acre farming company. At only 25 years old, I was a very young man with some field experience and a promising future.

In July 1993, I had finished my academic study and in August 1993, our university held a graduation ceremony in a fancy hotel to award our diplomas. During his speech, the dean of our university mentioned my name a couple of times. He mentioned my enthusiasm as a student, my commitment to my university, and my success in getting a good job very early in my career. My parents were thrilled with his speech and afterwards, when people were cheering me, I stood up and waved to everybody. When I sat down with my family, Mom was in tears. My dad stood up and kissed me, and so did Soraya. I was the only student mentioned in his speech and this also made me proud of myself and, for some reason, because of my new achievement and that unique moment, I felt like a tenacious man, just like my father. I also was happy to have Soraya beside me. With all of this excitement, I was certain that the new Santos generation would serve as examples of commitment, determination, tenacity, hard work and happiness.

Soraya and I continued dating for a long time despite living many miles apart. Then, the complaints started; she wanted to get married. She had always said that we loved each other and it didn't make any sense living apart. During our long distance relationship, we broke up at least twice. The second time, I thought that I would never see her again. But, I was totally wrong; it was only few weeks when my heart was telling that I was making a big mistake.

In May 1996, Soraya invited me to go to Mossoró, a city in the state of Rio Grande do Norte where she was finishing college. We rented a car and travelled a good distance to a deserted beach. Soraya had reserved a table for us at a restaurant with no TV and cell reception. We had such a romantic evening. We had a good bottle of wine and a fire pit outside our cozy place. A brilliant moon reflecting dazzling moonbeams on the sea water added to the romantic mood of the evening. It was then that we realized that we could not live apart much longer.

After that very pleasant surprise, we spent a few more months apart, but more united in our love. In November 1996, instead of going to Mossoró, I invited Soraya to come to Petrolina. Now, it was my time "to pay her back" with a surprise. Before she arrived, I went to the best restaurant in town and arranged for the *maître d'* to reserve a table with flowers and a bottle of champagne. From the airport, we headed directly to the restaurant. On our way, she questioned:

"Why aren't we going to your home?"

"I have a surprise for you."

Silence took over my automobile. So, I went on:

"How was your trip?"

"It was fine, but I am not interested in talking about that. You are making me nervous. I want to know where we're going. Come on, tell me…"

"It's a surprise, so I can't tell you. Relax and you will see."

Again, silence dominated our ride.

At the restaurant, she got more anxious. At this time, I was still living with my parents and she argued.

"Is something wrong with your parents? Can't I stay at your home? Don't they like me anymore?"

"You are something, aren't you? Relax, it has nothing to do with my parents. They are fine with you and they are expecting you later this evening."

Phew! Finally, we're on the elevator at the restaurant. I was feeling like a real gentleman escorting Soraya to announce a surprise that would change our lives forever. When the elevator door opened and the *maître d'* escorted us to our special table, a big smile appeared on her face. The dim lighting, the flowers, and the sparkling bottle of champagne were quite impressive. Her kisses came easily and were plentiful. Things were going well, and I was about to surprise her even more. After our waiter opened the champagne, I reached into my pocket as we were taking our first sip of champagne:

"Will you marry me?"

She was in tears and yelled. "Yes, yes, and yes. I love you so much."

After our unforgettable romantic time, we went back to my parents' home and there, my mom had prepared a second dinner to celebrate our engagement.

We got married on December 6, 1997, in Soraya's hometown, Fortaleza.

We set up our household soon in 1998, living in a furnished, paid-off apartment, owning our own car, and having a daily housekeeper, along with everything else that you need for a comfortable start. Then, in mid-1999, we got some great news. Soraya was pregnant. Our excitement was tempered when Soraya almost lost the baby twice. This pregnancy was so difficult that Soraya's doctor, Dr. Erika, told her to choose between her work and her pregnancy. So, she stopped working. We even had to sell our third-floor apartment when Soraya could no longer go up and down the steps. So, we bought a house instead.

Since the pregnancy was so difficult, we wanted to be close to Soraya's family for the delivery. Her parents, Arquimedes and Gardenia, were living in Fortaleza. So two months before the delivery, I drove her to Fortaleza for the rest of her pregnancy. I continued working in Petrolina and I often drove the 540 miles to Fortaleza when I could get away. Despite the difficult pregnancy, tests indicated that the fetus was completely normal and we also found out that it was a boy. So, we could now choose a name, which was a huge responsibility because, for me, choosing a name is very important. It can affect a kid all through adulthood. It can affect self-esteem; it also gives that first important impression to others. So, we chose the name Vinicius, meaning "Grape Grower," a name from my profession.

Hopeful are the days when you are expecting something that will bring you great joy. Even though your life will never again be your own, you know that it will be happier. This, for me, is the feeling of waiting for the birth of our baby.

On April 25, 2000, at 12:10 pm, Vinícius Bucar Lages Nogueira Santos was born, completely healthy. Our joy was indescribable as we watched our baby grow. He would mumble something like "pa pa, mam mam," then he learned to walk and each day our love for him grew, as did our commitment. We could only think about our baby, his comfort, his health and his future. When Vinicius was born, I owned a company and a small farm with a partner, a man who has been my friend since fifth grade. Our company was focused on assisting agribusiness clients. We were also planting grapes and mangoes on our farm.

In 2000 when Vinicius was born, Brazil's agri-business struggled because of a massive recession in the banking industry and credit was severely limited. Because of this recession, I needed to find a new livelihood. After all, my obligations had doubled and I could not afford to wait for the banks to recover.

Shortly thereafter, we learned that Soraya was pregnant again. This unplanned, but wonderful, news was soon followed by more good news.

An opportunity came up for me to work for an irrigation company. With some difficulty, I adapted to a new phase of my career. With my consulting business continuing and my new job, our lives began to return to a time of financial stability.

But, we didn't know that a great change in our lives was looming on the horizon.

CHAPTER 5

A NEW LIFE

The anguish had a grip on my whole being

Although we feared that the problems with the first pregnancy would be repeated, we were ecstatic to see that this one was going perfectly. I was thrilled; everything was wonderful. Soraya shared my enthusiasm and her only concern was to redecorate the room that would soon be shared by our two sons.

A couple of days before the scheduled delivery date, Soraya's mother came from Fortaleza to Petrolina to give us a hand. On January 18, 2002, at about noon, at the Memorial Hospital of Petrolina, our baby boy, Artur, was delivered by C-section. His size and weight were normal; his reflexes and other basic functions were tested…our second son was healthy. Soraya and I were delighted. Because of the C-section, Soraya spent another night in the hospital, but her condition was really very good. While still in the hospital, Artur ate for the first time, and, unlike his brother, Vinicius, who at first didn't take well to breastfeeding, he seemed to be a good eater.

Two days later, Vinicius and I went to the hospital to bring Artur and his mom home. When we got back to our house, we were really delighted to find that Edileuza, our housekeeper, and Maria, our babysitter, had done a great job organizing everything for our homecoming.

Artur's first night at home did not go well. Even though he had eaten well that day, he was fussy all night long. The following morning, my mother-in-law was alarmed, "Look! There are ants on Artur's dirty diapers. What's going on?"

Nobody paid much attention to this, so I asked Maria to just throw them out. His new room did have a strange sweet smell, but, for us, this was nothing.

By the third day, Artur's fussiness had become even worse, so Soraya and her mother took him to the doctor. Two doctors examined the baby and both thought he was just colicky, saying, "Take your baby home. He will be fine very soon."

This was just the beginning of the journey through a myriad of different diagnoses.

Back home, Artur was crying continuously, despite our constant efforts to comfort him. In fact, the more we touched him, the louder he cried. Since he had been eating regularly, Gardenia, my mother-in-law, had a thought. "Artur is a good eater, not like Vinicius, he must just be hungry."

Gardenia thought that Soraya didn't have enough breast milk to satisfy Artur's hunger. So, we supplemented it with a full bottle of infant formula. Proving that Gardenia was right, Artur drank the whole bottle and almost immediately fell into a deep sleep. Unfortunately, only a couple hours later, he suddenly awoke, crying so loudly and forcefully that it was almost as if he was being shocked.

After a half-day of work, I went home for lunch, where Gardenia told me,

"Look, I'm very worried about this baby. Two doctors checked him today and nothing was resolved. What should we do? I don't think we should take him to another doctor now. Besides, including Artur, we are exhausted, and we need a good rest."

Relying on her experience, I took her advice. Later that day, she said something that would have a great impact on Artur's life.

CHAPTER 6

THE SPASMS

A mother speaks for her baby, but the doctors do not always hear her

Gardenia and I discussed Artur's condition.

Gardenia said, "Look Idário, I '**disdice**' (it is an old fashioned way to say in Portuguese that you have changed your mind or what you just said is not worth it). Now, I think that we have to take Artur to the clinic. I don't agree with his doctor. I am worried that he is going to get worse."

"But, you just said that we shouldn't take him to the doctor," I said.

"Yes, but now I've changed my mind (**'I disdice'**). I think we must take him to the doctor."

Once again, Gardenia's opinion ruled. I went to work and Soraya and Gardenia took Artur to the clinic. At three o'clock, I got a call from Gardenia telling me to come to the clinic immediately. That's all she said! I imagined that something serious had happened to Soraya because she still had had no rest since the C-section. When I arrived at the clinic, Soraya was frantic. "Idário, we must admit Artur in the hospital. The doctor thinks that he might have a neurological problem."

This news completely floored me. I had no idea what a neurological problem was. The pediatrician wanted to readmit our baby into the same hospital where he was born and also recommended that Artur be seen by a neonatologist. Later on, we met with the doctor who would examine our baby. Throughout this time, Artur was fussy, irritated, crying, and he was not eating at all. Based on a previous examination, the doctor suspected an electrolyte imbalance, where she ordered an IV for him. By then, Artur was in his fourth day of life. That evening, our little King had visibly weakened and started having uncontrollable spasms. During these spasms, he would thrust his arms and legs upwards while arching his back, as if trying to get some relief. All the while, he cried constantly. These spasms would last for about one minute or so. After each episode, he became calm, his arms and legs relaxing, and he would fall asleep for few minutes. Then, he would repeat the cycle of spasms over and over.

Only one person did not see the cycles, the doctor. Each time she approached, Artur did not move. Gradually, he became more lethargic and, in his fifth day of life, was motionless, with spasms occurring at a much lower frequency.

What can we do? Why is our child going through all this? These questions pounded in my head. And I had no answers.

For me, there was only persistence. I always knew that tenacity was the key to great achievements, as evidenced in my dad's life. We should always be firm and never give up at the first sign of difficulty. Furthermore, we need to be focused and see things from many different perspectives. In critical situations, we must be mentally alert in order to make the best choices and make intelligent decisions.

I knew all of this, but I had no idea what was coming. *How could I use this ideology here?*

So, I pushed the doctors, forcing them to give me a diagnosis. With some pressure on the hospital board of directors, we scheduled a medical consultation. Several hours later, at least five doctors were beside my son's crib. We were expecting that one of these doctors would be a neonatologist, but instead, a neurologist showed up. During this conference, I kept silent, observing the scenario and beginning to feel that these experts had no idea what was wrong with my son. The neurologist came with a hammer-like instrument to test reflexes; the instrument was almost Artur's size! I noticed that this doctor seemed embarrassed when he began his examination. I assumed that he had never examined a newborn. He immediately put down the instrument and began to check my son's reflexes with his bare hands. Tapping on Artur's knees and elbows joints, the doctor was looking for some kind of neurological reaction.

For the entire consultation, Artur didn't move at all, so Soraya repeatedly tried to explain to the doctors what was happening during these spasms, but they were not paying any attention. It seemed to me that they only wanted to talk to each other. Logically, a mother speaks for her baby, but during this conference, it was like Soraya wasn't even there.

The doctors' failure to listen to Soraya infuriated me, but I remained silent. Interestingly, one doctor in the group was behaving like me; she didn't open her mouth. She just stood there without offering any opinion about the case.

I thought - This one, yes, she must suspect something that the others do not.

CHAPTER 7

DO ANGELS EXIST?

A mother should be able to hold her child in her arms.

After the meeting, all of us were very concerned. Gardenia suggested that we take Artur to Fortaleza for better care. Without a doubt, Fortaleza would be a better medical center, and it was the city where Vinicius was born. And we knew some doctors down there. She mentioned Dr. Osmiro, who was Vinicius' pediatrician. We were exhausted. Soraya had fallen asleep and the wall clock was ticking three o'clock in the morning when the doctor who was quiet during our meeting came to see Artur.

When I tried to ask something, she asked for silence, telling me that she wanted to observe him for a while. Artur was still lethargic. After a couple of minutes, our little king had one of those spasms. Immediately, the doctor, like an angel sent from God, said.

"Are you able to take him out of here?"

I did not understand her, but she clarified:

"Take him to a big city, anywhere, with a better medical center."

"Sure, we can do that, either to Fortaleza or Recife. Why? What's wrong with our baby?"

"I'm not sure; it could be a neurological problem and will probably require tests that we cannot do here. It seems that these involuntarily movements are seizures. Who do you know in Fortaleza?" she said.

"We know Dr. Osmiro. He was our first son's pediatrician."

"I know him well. I did my fellowship with him. I can assure you that he is one of the best in Fortaleza."

The doctor continued her hospital rounds while Soraya and I waited anxiously for daylight. I headed to my parents' house at six o'clock, waking my father to tell him what had happened a few hours before and that we were taking Artur to Fortaleza for treatment. Gardenia and Soraya would take him by plane and I would drive my car with our housekeeper, Edileusa, and Vinicius.

Still half asleep, my father was thinking straighter than I was when he said: "You need to go on the airplane, too. Can't you see that you are not emotionally well enough to drive? Besides, you haven't slept for several days.

So, I took off for the hospital to tell Soraya about the plan. In the meantime, my father called all my brothers and my cousin, Rosa, and told them to meet us there, too. I went to wake up Gardenia and told her that the doctor agreed about transferring Artur and asked her to make arrangements to go to Fortaleza. We needed to leave as soon as possible.

At about eight o'clock, I returned to the hospital only to find a huge commotion between Soraya and Artur's primary doctor. She refused to discharge Artur in such a rush, pointing out that we were too distressed to make that decision. At this point, I had had enough, seeing my son hopelessly lying in his crib, I demanded that he be discharged immediately.

Just then, God gave us another 'angel'. With the approval of the hospital director, Dr. Etelvina, who was also on duty that morning, immediately understood the situation and took responsibility for releasing our baby.

Dr. Etelvina was concerned that Artur might have seizures during the flight. So, she pulled Gardenia aside and showed her what to do if they happened. Of course, I had to sign releases for this rather unorthodox procedure, but at that point, I signed off without even knowing just what it was.

My sister, Irenice, had been checking out the flights and finally returned to the hospital with our tickets. The only flight available for that day was scheduled for 6 pm. So, during the afternoon, we contacted Dr. Osmiro in Fortaleza who quickly agreed to take Artur as his patient. Finally, we were set to leave Petrolina. Or so we thought. When we arrived at the airport, the DAC, Brazil's air traffic regulators, asked for Artur's documents. He needed identification to get on the plane, but we didn't have his birth certificate; it wasn't even issued yet. To further complicate things, it was Sunday and government offices were not open. In Brazil, the common way to solve such a problem is called 'jeitinho Brasileiro'[*]. Somehow my brothers, Isnaldo and Ivaldo, solved the problem. I really have no idea how they did it. All I cared about was getting Artur on that plane.

Throughout all this chaos, Artur was completely peaceful. He never even moved, almost as if he was paralyzed. At 6:00 pm, we took off from Petrolina to Fortaleza with a scheduled stop in Juazeiro do Norte. When we had all settled onto the plane, everyone became a little calmer, except me. Having taken this flight several times before, I was familiar with its route that crossed the famous Araripe's Mountains, close to Juazeiro do Norte. The geography of this area causes dramatic changes in atmospheric pressure, creating turbulence so intense that it seems that the aircraft is going to fall apart. I was the only one aware of this possibility, but I didn't tell anyone. I just prayed and, to my astonishment, God guided us calmly to our landing in Juazeiro do Norte. After this brief layover, we took off for Fortaleza. When we claimed our luggage in Fortaleza's airport, we met up with all of Soraya's relatives and immediately headed to the Regional Hospital of Unimed.

The chaos was about to begin again.

Even though this hospital was covered by our health plan, they demanded an advance payment of five thousand reais (about US$2,500.00) before admitting Artur! This demand baffled me, so I argued, but to no avail. After going through the admission procedures with Dr. Ariosto, Soraya's friend and the doctor on duty, they spoke with Dr. Osmiro and decided to admit him to the Neonatal ICU.

We were shocked. This hospital was the polar opposite of the one in Petrolina. Clearly, this hospital was a relief. Procedures here were completely different. Understandably, we had to dress in gowns with masks; we had to scrub our hands and arms before getting close to Artur, all to avoid infections. And the doctors, they were totally different from the ones in Petrolina. They talked more with us, explaining what they are doing and why they were doing it.

I was exhausted. So, I went to Gardenia's house to take a break. Early the second morning in Fortaleza, I returned to the hospital to wait for Dr. Osmiro. He arrived at 6:00 am and thoroughly examined Artur after which he ordered a series of laboratory tests. Before he left, I asked,

"Why does he have to be in the NICU?"

He replied bluntly: "It is because he is in a coma. Didn't they tell you?"

"They" were the doctors from Petrolina. Later, a nurse confirmed that Artur was in a deep coma.

I loved that child so much and I couldn't do anything to save him.

My wife, who had just undergone a cesarean delivery, was now suffering even more. She still had to provide breast milk for Artur, filling the bottles via a painful, mechanical process and then feeding him via a nasal tube. Natural breastfeeding creates an essential connection between mother and baby, so Soraya felt terrible, and, to make things worse, she couldn't even hold Artur in her arms because of so much monitoring equipment attached to him. This was not fair to Soraya and I asked God to put a stop to her suffering.

For several weeks, Artur was in an incubator with a mass of wires connecting him to a bunch of strange, beeping devices. During this time, Artur never moved on his own; his only motion was when Soraya or the nurses turned him to help prevent bedsores. Despite this, he still developed scars on his head and back and lost all of his hair. It wasn't long until we became familiar with the equipment and also with the nurses' and doctors' schedules.

I was very worried about everything; I just wanted to take my son home.

My life became a shuttle between Petrolina and Fortaleza. My expenses were out of control, and I had to make some adjustments. So, instead of traveling from Petrolina to Fortaleza by airplane, I started travelling by bus. By plane, it took one hour and thirty minutes. However, the bus took 16 hours! The difference in price and my new financial situation did not allow me the luxury of flying.

This did not prevent me, however, from having many questions. In my long bus trips, I found time to read and reflect and, from time to time, I was talking to myself. What if my son died? How would Soraya react if things get worse?

In my despair, I just begged God. "My Lord, You are the One on whom I can count, and You're the only one who has direct answers to all sorts of problems. Please do not let me down, I beg You."

I wanted answers, but I only found more questions.

(*) -"jeitinho Brasileiro" is an expression for the way of doing things by circumventing rules and social conventions. It is a typically Brazilian method of social navigation where an individual can make emotional appeals or use blackmail, family ties, promises, rewards or money to obtain favors or to get an advantage (Knack).

CHAPTER 8

LEUKODYSTROPHY?

Babies use their mothers as their voices to say what is happening to them.

"Idario, you need to return to Fortaleza right away. Just after you left, we got bad news about Artur. The doctors say he has a very rare disease and that he will not live long. Since this news, Soraya has suffered a breakdown, fainted, and has been hospitalized. She's also bleeding from the C-section. The situation is not good here…"

I had just arrived from Fortaleza when I got this call from my mother-in-law.

"Gardenia, where did this diagnosis come from? I was there yesterday and nobody told me anything."

"Remember the new MRI that the doctor ordered yesterday? You went to the radiological center with Artur!"

"Yes," I said

"Well, this exam says that Artur has a disease called Leukodystrophy."

When I hung up the phone, I couldn't hold back the tears. I felt that the world was collapsing. After settling down, I pulled myself back together. My father was with me, and, seeing my tears, gently tried to console me. He gave me a glass of water and I explained to him what was going on. We planned my return to Fortaleza.

To occupy my mind, I decided to research this disease, Leukodystrophy. It is a congenital disease. The prefix, Leuko, means white. This disease causes a dystrophy of the white part of the brain, the myelin sheath. The myelin sheath degenerates quickly, resulting in a painful death. The myelin sheath can be compared to the rubber or plastic wrapping around electrical wire. Without this protection, the electrical wire will short-circuit and start a fire. In the human brain, the myelin sheath covers and protects the neurons. When the myelin sheath starts deteriorating, the person becomes paralyzed, followed by an agonizing death.

Online, I read as much as I could find about this disease, but nowhere were the initial spasms that Artur had had in his first days.

I also found that there are several types of Leukodystrophy, one of which is treated by using special oil known as **Lorenzo's Oil**. There is a movie of this same name that is about leukodystrophy, so I rented it. After watching it, I was convinced that this was not my son's disease; the symptoms didn't match with my son's. Regardless, this movie inspired me not to give up.

I needed to be much more persistent. Like Lorenzo's father in the film, I felt certain that my son didn't have this disease, and even if I was wrong, at least it could be treated with this oil. So, I took a deep breath and tried to move on.

The next day, I traveled to Fortaleza. Getting there, I met Gardenia, very sad.

"Things are so bad; the doctors are telling us that Artur's condition is hopeless. They want to send him home. The damage is done, and even if he does survive, he will not be normal," she said.

"Did she give you a written diagnosis?"

By my question, my mother-in-law reacted strangely and in anguish she told me.

'Do you think that we are giving up on Artur?"

"I did not say that! I just want to know if the doctor gave you a document saying that he has this disease."

"Actually, no. At one point, she even **disdice** (took back her words). After telling us about the disease, I was distraught and told her that we just couldn't lose Artur. At that, she said that she would investigate further, but she had no doubt, Artur had leukodystrophy."

In their despair, my wife's family could only begin grieving, not realizing that the doctor's diagnosis could have been wrong. So, I pushed on. Just like me trying to solve Artur's case, my brother-in-law, Arquimedes, a very smart man and a new attorney in Fortaleza, had also done an Internet research and had printed out hundreds of pages of information about leukodystrophy. Discussing our findings, we came to a conclusion: Artur's doctor did not listen to Soraya when she said that Artur had been born normally. This just reminded me of Vinicius's first pediatrician, who always says that babies use their mothers as interpreters to say what is happening to them.

I was convinced that I needed to have a second opinion.

Since only parents are allowed into this hospital's ICU, Artur was alone there and I was worried he might be feeling abandoned. Even though he was in a coma, I felt that his spiritual presence was very strong among us. I had never had such a feeling, but, when I was around him, I could feel that my little king had something divine around him. During these tough days, touching him was the only time that I could feel some peace.

Soraya had been sedated, but when she saw me, she fell apart, obviously in great despair. Trying to offer some comfort, I reminded her that the second opinion might give us some renewed hope. Besides, I had read about leukodystrophy and I was not convinced that our son had that disease.

I left Soraya to rest and went to see Artur. He was so helpless, there at the mercy of the unknown, as if waiting for God's miracle. For the first time, I felt that I could lose my child. Holding his tiny hands, I talked to him, thinking that my voice might be comforting. I told him to hang on and that I wouldn't stop until I solved this medical mystery.

Soraya was discharged that evening and we both went to Artur's room. Our fears of losing our baby or having him face life with handicaps were only growing. Soraya stayed with Artur while I went into the hallway to call my friend, Edilson, a very kind and spiritual man, the husband of my cousin Rose. I updated him on Artur's situation and asked for advice. I told him that I was a man of faith and that my prayers had not been answered; my son was still in grave danger.

Following his advice, I went back to the ICU and very gently, we put our hands inside the incubator and, touching Artur's head, I asked God,

"Dear God, I am not the most religious man nor can I pray as I wish I could. But I am a believer and if you, my Lord, want this boy, take him into your kingdom. But if you allow Artur to live with us, we promise to love and care for him to the best of our ability, regardless of his mental or physical condition."

I then turned my attention to my son and told him,

"Artur, if it is your desire to be with God, we will accept that. You will be in great hands. But if you want to stay with Mom and Dad, be sure that we'll love and support you in any circumstance, and don't forget that your brother, Vinicius, is waiting to play with you."

I felt energized and something inside me told me that good things were going to happen.

CHAPTER 9

WE NEED LIGHT

Nothing could discourage me; it was a matter of honor to solve this mystery

I slept for about 30 minutes then got up and went alone to the hospital for the 6:00 am appointment with the new doctor, the one with the second opinion.

A highly regarded neonatologist showed up, accompanied by Artur's primary doctor, to perform a lengthy examination and analysis of all of his test results. I closely followed their discussion. The new doctor was adamant that only one MRI test was not enough to diagnose Leukodystrophy. They disagreed about the interpretation of the MRI results. Even though I didn't completely understand their technical terms, it seemed that the new doctor, like me, was questioning the diagnosis. On one hand, Artur's primary physician thought that the myelin sheath, the white matter in the brain, was destroyed leading her to the leukodystrophy diagnosis. On the other hand, the consulting doctor could see some of the myelin sheath on Artur's brain, throwing doubt on that diagnosis. Meanwhile, I was solving the puzzle in my mind.

Light, more light. That is what I was looking for.

A series of new tests were ordered by the neonatal doctor. She seemed to be pursuing a specific course, but didn't reveal it to us. This investigation and discussion lasted about one hour. As she left the ICU, she asked me to wait for the test results.

Artur's primary doctor, however, told me she was still confident in her diagnosis, but also persuaded me to wait for the new results. I did not want to just sit still. So, I confronted her.

"Look, I'm no doctor, I have no money, and I am nobody. But if you think that this boy needs something, or needs to go somewhere else, anywhere in the world, for treatment, please tell me. I will find a way to do it."

Despite her certainty about the diagnosis, I was even more confident that a different one would be coming. I just had to work harder. So, instead of waiting for the new test results, I requested a copy of the MRIs to send to another city, Recife, for a third professional evaluation. But the hospital refused to give me a copy of the results! Furious, I went directly to the radiology lab that had done the MRI. There I met a radiologist who said,

"Have you ever taken pictures from the same camera, on the same day, and in the same environment? And, when you develop them, some pictures come out great and others are out of focus?"

He continued,

"Our equipment sometimes can be compared to single cameras. However, in a normal baby's brain, we can see a more defined white matter. Here, in your son's exams, instead of white, we see gray matter in his brain."

"So, are you convinced that my son has leukodystrophy?"

"**No**! I cannot confirm this diagnosis. That's why I put a question mark on this exam. Your doctor is the one to provide the diagnosis. Besides, as I told you, this is like a picture; it can be out of focus. We avoid repeating this procedure for newborns to minimize radiation exposure."

I thanked him and left his office still optimistic, but I was still sailing in turbulent seas. Back at home, I continued my research. I searched for hours for a disease with similar symptoms. I found lots of diseases, each one more horrible than the previous. In my deep thoughts I asked myself, *What if my son does not have leukodystrophy, but something even worse?* Despite my thoughts, nothing would drag me down; it was a matter of honor to solve the mystery that surrounded my little king. My positive way of thinking about my son turned into this: *Everyone (family and doctors) is working hard to get you out of this "box."*

After hours of researching, I fell asleep at the computer.

My phone ringing sounded like a siren! It was 6:00 am and I had only slept a couple of hours. Artur's primary doctor was on the line telling me to come to the hospital immediately. As I drove to the hospital, I could only think the worst. "Had Artur's condition deteriorated?" At the hospital, I found Artur the same, still lethargic, vital signs OK and no noticeable change.

Why I did I have to rush to the hospital? A few minutes later my concern subsided.

"Last night, I spoke to a doctor, a friend of mine in Sao Paulo, and he suggested that we run some new tests. They can all be done here except one that has to be done in Sao Paulo. I need you to deliver this material to a clinic here in Fortaleza. Then, come back and I'll have some blood samples ready for you to send to Sao Paulo."

I imagined that this was not a right procedure, but I did not hesitate in following her requests. At this point, I would do everything to have my son properly diagnosed.

Fortaleza was calm these days. It was Carnival time in Brazil and usually the traffic is crazy all over the country, but Fortaleza does not celebrate it. So, my first task was a "piece of cake." I dropped off the blood and urine samples and returned to the hospital. At my arrival, the physician instructed me about my new task.

"At noon, the other samples will be ready. They must be in my friend's hands in Sao Paulo today. So you'll need to send them by air. It's essential that he get this material today or else all of our work will be lost."

"I got it, Doctor! I'll get it there today even if I have to take an airplane and deliver the material personally!"

She opened a very thick book with a black cover and told me.

"One more thing, Dad. We suspect that Artur may have a metabolic disorder. So, I've suspended any breast milk for him just as a precaution."

Motioning toward the open book, she continued. "I'm ordering a revised diet immediately. I believe that this change will help him if he has one of these diseases. And if he doesn't, the new diet won't hurt."

"What do these diseases do to a baby?" I asked.

"Well, their metabolism does not function properly, creating a toxic condition. But, let's not anticipate anything right now. We first need the test results."

More anxious I asked: "*Can they be cured?*"

"Take it easy, it's too early to answer that. There are many types of metabolic disorders, more than you can imagine to be precise, and we are focused on three: Urea Cycle Disorder, Phenylketonuria and MSUD."

These three names were etched in my mind. Certainly, they were very strange to me, but it crossed my mind that things were beginning to make some sense.

Finally, there was some light!

CHAPTER 10

A KNIGHT OF THE ROUND TABLE

Nothing could stop me from reaching my goal

An odyssey typically consists of grandiose epic moments and great battles. But, in my case, it was a series of small fights where each fight was always pushing to disrupt my focus on the goal. On behalf of my King Artur, like the mythological king, I was the devoted knight willing to do anything to win this war. There would be no dragon, warriors, or mere agents of bureaucracy that would block my quest for the Grail - in my case, the diagnosis of the disease and the cure for my son.

Nothing could stop a Knight of the Round Table, and that was how I felt. My mission: to deliver my son's blood sample in São Paulo.

Sao Paulo is about 1,400 miles from Petrolina and flying there at the last minute would cost a fortune. But that's just what I was about to do when I recalled that my friend, Hiroshi Imagawa, lived in Sao Paulo. Maybe he could help me. Hiroshi is a Japanese businessman working for Sansuy Corporation. We were first business associates, but soon became close friends. I knew that he had just returned to Sao Paulo from an international irrigation exposition in Petrolina. So I called him, and after summarizing my story, asked for his help with our mission. Without hesitation, he agreed to help. Hiroshi's willingness to do this big favor was something beyond kindness.

Finally, I had the samples in hand, so I took off for the International Pinto Martins Airport with Soraya's sister, Sylvana.

A quick aside...these complicated steps were possible due to all the support coming from my and Soraya's families. Sylvana in particular was especially wonderful throughout this whole ordeal. She had been studying in the USA, and when she returned to Brazil, she didn't know that Artur was in a coma. When she learned of Artur's situation, she never wavered in her dedication to us. Clearly, her love for him was unconditional. I have no words to express my gratitude to her. Only God knows what would have happened to Soraya and our baby without Sylvana's help.

At the airport, I saw that the only flight to Sao Paulo that would work for us was on TAM airlines. So, Sylvana and I headed to TAM's package terminal only to find that no more packages could be accepted for the flight we wanted. We had missed the deadline by a few minutes! I pleaded with the shipping agent, explaining the urgency of the situation, but he couldn't do anything for me. The flight was closed. But for me, it wasn't closed! Ignoring the "no access" sign, I opened the gate to TAM's shipping facility and started walking without any idea what I was going to do. At this, the agent tried to stop me, threatening to call the police. His threat did not faze me. All I knew was that my package needed to be on this flight!

As I tramped through this vast building, not sure what I would find, a person in authority, probably the department manager, approached me in an intimidating way, wanting to know what was going on. Trying to be calm but with little success, I explained to him why I had "crossed the line" into this "employees only" area. Unlike the agent out front, this gentleman listened to my story and realized the importance of my request. Again, it seemed like divine intervention. He immediately called the same agent who had denied me earlier and ordered him to dispatch my package on that day's flight. Finally calming down a bit, I let the doctor know that the package was finally on its way.

Our hopes for Artur were in that precious package on its way to Sao Paulo.

CHAPTER 11

MSUD?

Finally, God, in his mercy, had answered our prayers

I was in the ICU with Artur. I could swear I saw his left arm move, but discounted it as a product of my imagination. He hadn't moved for days. Soraya was talking to the nurses and didn't notice anything. So, I didn't bother to even tell anybody.

Back home, I sat in front of the computer, the only activity that really calmed me down. It was as if, when looking through countless websites, I unraveled mazes that could lead me to the most important reward, to see my son cured.

Urea Cycle Disorder, Phenylketonuria and MSUD. It was amazing how lacking the Portuguese websites were about metabolic disorders. And what information I could find really didn't explain anything. With the Google tool that automatically translates from one language to another, I began to browse the English websites where I found a wealth of useful information.

Of the three diseases mentioned by the doctor, one got my attention: MSUD, Maple Syrup Urine Disease. Researching it was like reading a page-turner, a book that I couldn't put down. The early signs of this disease were so similar to Artur's first few days.

I was at the beginning of the maze, but it was time to visit my son in the ICU.

Did he really move his arm? This question kept invading my mind. As if in answer to my question, the unexpected happened. For sure this time, our little king moved his arm. Just to make sure, I put my hand inside the incubator and touched him. He reacted to my touch. I called Soraya.

"You won't believe it; Artur just moved his arm. Come and see!"

With this seemingly miraculous revelation, my joy was matched by my concern. I felt that he was suffering from this MSUD, but I didn't really know what it was. Artur moved again. Tearfully, Soraya shouted to the nurses. "Come, look at him; Artur moved his arm!"

After many days of sadness and uncertainty, I finally could see a vibrant look on Soraya's face and was confident that our baby seemed to be heading in a better direction.

When we got married, I had some doubt whether she would be a good mother, or even a good partner. I believed that she also thought the same about me. But with our lives unfolding as they were, I realized that I had made a wonderful choice. Soraya is a sincere person, very polite, friendly and with great integrity. No one would choose to have a child with the problems that Artur had, but she seemed to be the perfect mother for such a child. Her dedication and love for her son was beyond human limits. These traits endeared her to other people, naturally attracting them to her side. She was always surrounded by supportive family and friends, and, by now, these friends included the ICU staff. So, Artur, despite the coma, was pampered there like he was royalty.

A Special woman for a Special cause – Soraya Bucar – Synonymous of strength and perseverance

We often rank things on a scale from one to ten, with ten being the absolute best. In the case of Soraya, as a wife, a mother, and a friend to all, she far outshines even the absolute best in my eyes. Soraya has exceeded all expectations that a man can have of a woman and a child can have of a mother. Super Soraya, mother of "King" Artur and "Sir" Vinícius; this is the way that I define this amazing trio that came into my life to teach me how to pursue happiness.

Artur moved again and again, almost like he was showing off. Everybody was delighted. Meanwhile, more questions ran through my mind: Does this change relate to his new diet? It seems that it probably did because that is the only thing that had changed since he went into this coma. Still, I didn't know if he had leukodystrophy or a metabolic disorder.

I was so anxious to get to the computer and continue my research. Arriving at Gardenia's house, a euphoric Soraya was shouting to everyone that Artur had moved his arm.

Arquimedes was there, even more excited than us! He had asked his cousin, Moises, if we could use his office, which had a better high-speed Internet connection. The three of us became a team of researchers, all focusing on MSUD. After only minutes of searching, I found a website explaining pretty much everything about MSUD. It was unbelievable; everything I read there seemed as if Artur was the subject. Without noticing, tears were streaming down my cheeks. Moises asked why I was crying. I told him that I was sure that Artur suffered from this disease.

In loud voice, I read for my loyal friends, "MSUD is a hereditary disease caused by a deficiency of an enzyme involved in amino acid metabolism. This deficiency manifests itself in the urine giving off a sweet smell, thus, Maple Syrup Urine Disease." In addition to never having heard of this disease, I also had no clue what this maple syrup substance was. We don't have it in Brazil. I further found that the three amino acids, leucine, isoleucine, and valine, cannot be metabolized and, therefore, build up in the blood to the detriment of proper brain function. "Untreated MSUD can cause mental retardation, physical disabilities, and death."

I took a deep breath and continue my reading. "Maple Syrup Urine Disease describes a variety of disorders. The symptoms of classic MSUD are usually evident within the first week of life and include a poor appetite, irritability, and the characteristic sweet odor of the urine. Within days, the infants may lose their sucking ability, grow listless, have a high-pitched cry, and become limp with episodes of rigidity."

I paused to tell Arquimedes and Moises that this last characteristic was evident in Artur right before he fell into the coma. I continued:

"Without diagnosis and treatment, symptoms progress rapidly to seizures, a coma, and death. Milder forms of MSUD are possible also, but even then, the symptoms can be severe during an unrelated illness, such as the flu or an infection, and lead to a metabolic crisis. In variant, milder forms, the child's first symptom may simply be not acting like a normal, happy kid."

Treatment involves a special diet and the monitoring of protein intake. The special diet omits any food containing the three branched-chain amino acids; these essential acids are then added back to the diet in a form that can safely be absorbed. Close medical care is critical because even mild illnesses can become life-threatening and require hospitalization.

Each parent of a child with MSUD carries a defective recessive gene for MSUD along with a normal gene. Parents are called "carriers" and are not affected by the disorder. Each child with MSUD has received one defective gene from each parent.

When both parents are carriers, there is a 1 in 4 chance with each pregnancy that the baby will receive a defective gene from each parent and, therefore, have MSUD; a 2 in 4 chance the baby will receive one defective and one normal gene, thus becoming a carrier of MSUD and not actually have the disease; and a 1 in 4 chance the baby will receive two normal genes. Persons with two normal genes cannot pass MSUD to their offspring...."

I was quite certain that I had found Artur's problem, so our next goal was to research if there were any known cures. We immediately hit a wall. Arquimedes found out that MSUD has no cure; however, treatment based on a strict diet and a very expensive formula free of amino acids was available. We raced home with this news.

Early the next morning at the hospital, I met with Artur's doctor and told her that I had researched the metabolic disorders and that I was sure Artur had MSUD. I offered her my research findings. At this, she was rather abrupt, saying that I was being too hasty and that the lab results would tell the story.

I agreed with her that the test results were the key. However, she didn't seem to appreciate my efforts to try to help to solve this mystery. It would seem that she, too, was hasty in diagnosing leukodystrophy. I couldn't blame her, though, for her first approach and I felt that her intentions were always good. But there must have been questions in her mind as she decided to suspend the diet of breast milk while ordering some special formula from the United States. This new diet seemed to have a positive impact on him. Now, he was regularly moving both arms and one of his legs, a dramatic change from his earlier condition. If you hadn't seen him in this paralyzed state, these movements would not have been noteworthy. But for Soraya and me, they were extraordinary and more than enough to tell us that we were no longer adrift.

My research and observations of Artur were making this complicated chess game become more clear and I was now certain that I had just made a checkmate.

Right then, I finally felt that my little king was returning to us.

It was like a rebirth.

CHAPTER 12

MSUD - FOR SURE

If I knew then what I know now, my son would not have suffered as much as he did.

"Your son has Maple Syrup Urine Disease, more commonly known as **MSUD**. Children with this disease produce urine with a smell similar to maple syrup, a very sweet, thick liquid made from the sap from maple trees. It's common at breakfast as a sweet topping for pancakes in the U.S. and Canada. It's not popular here, but that's how this disease got its name. The formula that Artur's taking now is for children with this disorder. He should respond to it favorably. However, he's been in a coma for so long, we can't begin to know the extent of damage he may have experienced. Brain damage is always possible in these situations…"

The lab results had arrived from Sao Paulo. Artur's physician had just reported this final diagnosis. Although the explanation was rather terse, her words did not surprise me. I now could see more pieces of this puzzle coming together. When we first brought Artur home, right after his birth, his room had a sweet aroma that I noticed most when I was close to him. And my mother-in-law had noticed some ants gathering on the dirty diapers. It was strange seeing ants there, but what did we know about this! Now, I realized that the ants were actually after this sweet syrup.

If I had known sooner! If I only knew that sweet scent I noticed coming from my son's urine was related to MSUD. If I only had paid attention when we saw ants in his used diapers!

We were so relieved. The formula was obviously helping him. Artur was getting better. At least, for now, he was acting more and more like a normal baby. However, what were the longer term treatment options? I doubted that the doctor even knew. But, based on my research, I knew MSUD could not be cured, so what would his future be?

With the situation in Fortaleza calming down a bit, I had to get back to my work in Petrolina. But as soon as I arrived there, Soraya called me, distressed, saying that the doctor was preparing to discharge Artur.

"It has been only two days since Artur's diagnosis. How could she possibly want to discharge him? Isn't he still in the incubator? And how can we deal with this gastro feeding tube and the formula? Is it even available for us to buy?" I practically yelled into the phone.

Of course, I didn't expect Soraya to have answers for these questions. I was just frustrated. She just asked me to come back to Fortaleza right away.

Meanwhile, Sylvana had contacted a physician in Belo Horizonte. This doctor apparently knew about a similar case in a city of Caicó also in Ceará State, not too far from Fortaleza. In her intensive investigation, fortunately, Sylvana found Mr. Giovanni. When he heard about Artur, he called immediately and spoke with Sylvana and Arquimedes, telling them his daughter's story. She also suffered from MSUD. He also asked me to call him, emphasizing, "Artur's father can call me at any time."

Giovanni was very helpful when we talked. With great empathy, he slowly explained to me what problems this disease could cause. We spoke for more than two hours. He advised me to immediately contact his daughter's doctors. They could help Artur. Finally, I asked a key question.

"What would you do if Artur were your son?"

He responded with conviction.

"I know, you see that your son is improving, but it's very likely that his amino acid levels are still very high. These acids are toxic to him. His system is being poisoned and he needs medical care by qualified doctors. You can't find this in Fortaleza. Take him immediately to Porto Alegre or Natal where I know there are doctors who have some experience with MSUD. And don't hesitate; the toxins in his system must be promptly treated to avoid brain damage. Try Natal first. I just heard that my daughter's doctors admitted a little baby there named Islany and she has MSUD as well. They are the only doctors in our region dealing with this disease."

Giovanni gave me the names and numbers of two doctors, one in Porto Alegre – Rio Grande do Sul State and one in Natal – Rio Grande do Norte. When I started to thank him for all his help, he stopped me, saying.

"You don't need to thank me. My only request of you is that you **do the same for someone else as I am doing for you**. And if you go to Natal, let me know, so I can meet you there."

At that, I pledged to myself to honor his request.

CHAPTER 13

IN DIRE STRAITS

We just wanted a peaceful moment

How many tests would he have to endure? Every time we had our hopes up, a dark cloud would appear. Each time the exit to this maddening maze was in sight, another wall materialized out of nowhere. With so many challenges, even a knight of the Round Table would wilt. However, King Artur's strength gave me the energy to continue and to form an unbreakable chain of family and friends.

I truly feel that there was something magical about Artur during this odyssey. He had been in a coma. He couldn't talk or express himself in any way. Nonetheless, I could sense such a strong spirituality about him. He seemed to send out an aura that made me stronger and more determined to continue fighting for him. I began to see the world differently and act differently. I had been a hotheaded guy, losing my temper easily. Now, I was calmer and more thoughtful, a nicer person, I think. I came to realize that he didn't come to us by accident. He was a gift that would give meaning to our lives.

After my conversation with Giovanni, the man whose daughter had MSUD, my head was spinning. We needed to act quickly. I called Arquimedes to fill him in. I told him about the toxicity of the acids in Artur's system and that it was urgent to have him examined by an MSUD specialist. Everyone agreed that Sylvana should contact the doctor in Natal. She also contacted Dr. Ricardo Pires in Porto Alegre who agreed to take him, too, but cautioned us that the longer trip to Porto Alegre could compromise the situation. Although he didn't have an infection at the time, Artur was already weak and such a trip could be dangerous for him. In his opinion, it would be better if we took Artur first to Natal, rehabilitate him and then, if necessary, bring him to Porto Alegre.

At that, the doctor recommended that Artur should travel to Natal by special medical air transport.

Another wall materialized.

As we were preparing to move Artur the next day, we were dealt another blow. Despite Dr. Bosco's orders, UNIMED, our health insurer, refused to provide the air transport to Natal, although we had a right to this service, claiming that the hospital in Fortaleza was providing good care. He definitely was getting good care; however, it was not the proper treatment for him. I even tried to emphasize to UNIMED what the doctor from Natal had confirmed and what Mr. Giovanni had told me that delaying the right care could be causing irreversible brain damage. The health insurer's representative who we talked to on the phone didn't even know what this disease was! She was rude and inflexible, obviously concerned only about her company's profitability.

Proving a popular saying that "justice delays, but never fails," Arquimedes worked all night long preparing a petition to sue UNIMED, which he filed the next day.

The Brazilian justice system is known as a turtle on its run; however, thanks to Arquimedes, it didn't take long for it to decide in our favor. On the same day, the judge demanded that within 14 hours UNIMED make available the necessary transportation for Artur. Any delay would result in a penalty of BRL$50,000 (about US$25,000) daily.

The court's order also included the requirement that Artur be transferred to Porto Alegre after his rehabilitation in Natal. Fearful that UNIMED would appeal the judge decision and delay the transfer, I asked Arquimedes to buy commercial airplane tickets from Fortaleza to Natal for Gardenia, Artur, Sylvana, and Soraya. I was about to get on a plane to go from Petrolina to Natal when I learned that UNIMED would not appeal the decision; however, their aircraft was in maintenance in Sao Paulo and would not be available in Fortaleza for another two days. This sounded like an excuse to me. So, I decided to take the risk, moving Artur by commercial aircraft. Lowering the amino acids levels as quickly as possible was the priority for Artur and the doctors in Fortaleza were not able to help him. A couple of hours later, my son was hospitalized in Natal.

The doctor from Natal told us that we should be patient and that the planned dialysis treatment would be his rebirth. Even though the risks of this procedure were significant, he was confident that it would be successful and that Artur would come out of it a different baby. Showing some pictures, Dr. Bosco briefly explained the process:

"The peritoneal dialysis (PD) will clean your son's blood and remove extra fluids using one of his body's own natural filters, known as the peritoneal membrane. The peritoneal membrane is the lining that surrounds the peritoneal cavity, which is in the abdomen and contains the stomach, spleen, liver, and intestines. During the PD process, a solution will be pumped into the peritoneum through a catheter and the peritoneal membrane will act as a filter and draw waste from his blood into the solution. Once the solution has absorbed the waste acids, it is drained through the catheter and replaced with fresh solution."

So many complicated words! So many hopes!

Our hopes were confirmed when we had a chance for the first time to meet another family dealing with MSUD. It was a great chance for me to get more information and make sure that we were in good hands. Giovanni told me the baby girl, Yslani, had been diagnosed on her sixth day of life, so her treatment was started early and brain damage could be mitigated. Her parents obviously were joyous. They were very confident with the doctors from Natal and confirmed that our son was in great hands. Certainly, they were very happy to leave the hospital with their daughter.

I was so happy for them, but could only think of all that we had gone through; three hospitals in three states, so many doctors and so much time, now more than a month. Yslani's parents definitely inspired me, but I knew that we were still in an uphill battle.

Compared to Fortaleza, the ICU at Memorial Hospital of Natal had a more restricted visitation policy. It started at 9:00 am and continued through 9:00 pm and allowed only one visitor at a time. At least, any family member could visit, not just the parents. The dialysis procedure took place during that first night without any of us there since it was happening during non-visitation hours.

After spending an anxious night, we went straight to the ICU in the morning. As we headed directly into Artur's room, the doctor on duty told me that the procedure was going as planned, but cautioned me.

"I must warn you. The scene in Artur's room will be very upsetting. He is covered with tubes attached to machines. Just try to be calm and realize that this is essential for his survival. He might be suffering a little now, but, in couple of days, he will be much better."

As the doctor was finishing her warning, I could hear Artur's cry. I'll never forget the scene as I entered the room. Artur was wailing in pain, tears streaming down his face, as he desperately trembled back and forth as if trying to ease his own suffering. In tears, I could barely look at him. How was it possible that, yesterday, this baby could be so lethargic and today be crying so hard and moving his tiny body like this…?

Just then, unbelievably, he suddenly paused his wailing and shaking, fixed his eyes on me, his spirit clearly visible, and spoke, not verbally, but with his eyes. "Dad, get me out of here, I can't deal with this anymore. Don't let mom see me."

I was astonished. Although he did not speak, I could actually feel these words. Nothing like that had even happened to me before. Looking for strength, I wiped my tears, touched his hands, and promised that he would be well soon and everything would be fine.

The dialysis procedure was horrific. Artur was surrounded by pumping machines and electronic monitoring devices. Inserted just below his belly button, there was a ½ inch diameter catheter. Like a valve, this catheter had a little device on its end, which allowed the nurses to reverse the liquid flow. Via flexible tubes, this catheter was connected on one end to a gallon bag containing a special solution. And on the other end, it was connected to a large waste container collecting my son's body fluids. I could pretty much figure out how the dialysis worked. The yellowish solution was slowly pumped into Artur via the catheter. It circulated through his body and was discharged into the waste container with a more darkish tinge, obviously picking up the toxins in his body. As the doctor explained, the solution absorbed the non-metabolized amino acids as it passed through his body, flushing them out of his system. The solution caused his belly to inflate like a big balloon ready to explode, causing his legs and face to almost disappear into his bloated torso.

He had been on this dialysis for about 12 hours and the procedure would last for at least 60 more. It seemed like torture, but it was the only way to cleanse him. The pain must have been unbearable for him. He seemed so desperate and his suffering was killing me.

This whole situation was frightening. I only wanted to drag him out of the incubator and take him home. He was struggling so much that my earlier optimism was fading; I felt I was losing him.

The others were waiting for me outside the ICU. I knew I had to report to them, but I didn't want anyone, especially Soraya, to go in there and see him in this condition. I am definitely not a good actor. Coming out of the ICU, I told Soraya that everything was OK and Artur was asleep. She didn't buy that, so I went on, trying to bar the entrance to the room with my arms and saying that the nurses were working with him and they didn't want anyone inside. This didn't work either. She pushed my arms aside and rushed into the ICU. Moments later, the nurse in the room with Artur called for help. Soraya had fainted, landing on the floor. As a result, she had to be admitted to the hospital. Her C-section was bleeding again and she was unconscious.

What a terrible day! Little over a month since my son's birth and we had not had one minute of peace and calm. And we still were worried about losing him. Back and forth between the ICU and Soraya's hospital room, I didn't know where to turn. When visitation ended at 9:00 pm, I had to leave my son with this painful agony and went to Soraya's room. To my surprise, my wife has being discharged. We went to our hotel and could do nothing but pray.

How many days as terrible as this one will we still have to face?

We're not aware of how extensive our odyssey would become.

CHAPTER 14

NEW HOPE

We thank God for always giving us new hope

Each day, I thought I had more ability to absorb the unforeseen brutal strikes. Each day, my strength seemed to diminish with each new bit of bad news. Then, the next morning, I hear from the hospital, *"Your son had a stroke during the night! We were able to revive him, and he's responding well to treatment, but his situation is very critical."*

At this, my concern for Artur was momentarily surpassed by my complete astonishment. This disastrous news was bad enough, but the hospital hadn't even called us in during the night to come in and be with Artur. He could have died! Regaining control of my emotions, I abandoned any thoughts of confronting the doctor about this obvious mistake. Instead, I rushed in to see my son. Our **king** was very pale; it seemed that they had sedated him. He was not moving at all.

And his rebirth, when would it happen? Is that not what the doctor had promised after dialysis?

I had so many doubts. My intuition was that we were being tested again. Artur had survived so many awful days, so perhaps God and his angels were apparently not abandoning him. When I told Soraya what happened, she, naturally, was distraught, but didn't faint again. Instead, she went to see our son and came out even more worried.

When Artur's dialysis ended, his transformation was amazing. Dr. Bosco had been right; we had never seen him like this. Lying in his incubator, Artur would follow me with his eyes as I moved about. He reacted to noises, like objects dropping to the floor. He moved almost like a normal baby. It seemed improbable that he could be either blind or deaf, as the doctors in Fortaleza had warned. After a couple more days, Artur was transferred out of the ICU and into a regular hospital room. Unfortunately, on the same day that Artur was transferred, Yslani was readmitted to the hospital, in the room right next to Artur. Her parents told us that she had an infection.

I recalled that the infections can aggravate this disease.

During their ordeals, Artur and Yslani had to be fed through a feeding tube because they had lost the ability to suck. So Dr. Bosco now recommended that we get a speech therapist to try to help them regain this ability. Since our health insurance wouldn't cover such therapy, Yslani's father and I negotiated a deal with a therapist, Dr. Lourdes, to work with both kids.

Dr. Lourdes evaluated Artur on her first visit and told us that it would be very hard for him to recover his sucking ability. The nerves and muscles of Artur's mouth were not reacting to any stimulation. She told us that she never had a case like this. Even so, she prescribed a medication that we should get for her next visit.

Dr. Lourdes was not only a skilled therapist, but she also worked with passion. After working with Artur on that first day of actual therapy, she immediately realized that he would need at least two sessions per day. Without hesitation, I agreed with her. I really had no option, but I had no idea how I would pay her. I was, quite literally, broke. Right after that session, I called my dad and asked him for help and he readily agreed. His generosity temporarily eased my concerns, but I still knew that I was heading to a financial "black hole."

Small miracles were helping to sustain Soraya and me. Even to Dr. Lourdes' surprise, the therapy seemed to be working. Artur accelerated his mouth movements and sucked half of the formula in the bottle until he was exhausted and fell into a deep sleep. Talk about small miracles! We were all in tears, including Dr. Lourdes. She had never seen such an effort by a baby to drink. From this day, her commitment to Artur only grew. She was not only his doctor; she was treating him as her own son.

During our prayers, we thanked God for giving us this new hope.

CHAPTER 15

A TRAGEDY

For those who have MSUD, a simple cold can be a death sentence

Our contingent of supporters was about to grow larger. Later that day, we met the Fernandes family, Eimard, Andreza, and their five-year-old son, João Victor, who also had MSUD. João Victor was remarkable. He had no outward signs of the disease and seemed to be a very smart boy. He attended a regular school and he even sang a song for us. His parents were very nice. Seeing João Victor, I felt hopeful that Artur could one day be just like him. We talked for hours as they shared their MSUD experience with us. The Fernandes' problems, in particular, pretty much mirrored ours. They encouraged us to go to Dr. Ricardo in Porto Alegre.

From that first meeting, the Fernandes family supported us, taking turns visiting us every day, bringing us food, and sometimes they would do our laundry. What a blessing they became for us. And their testimony about their struggle with MSUD had invigorated me. As my understanding of this terrible disease became greater, I began to feel more confident in dealing with Artur's condition and my commitment to fight for him became even stronger.

To our great relief, Artur's condition was improving each day. Unfortunately, Yslani was only getting worse, so bad that she had to be transferred from her hospital room into the ICU. The infection was apparently the problem. I wondered…she had been diagnosed so early and had been treated from the start by doctors experienced in MSUD. Artur had had a lot of complications and was now getting better. What on earth was happening with Yslani?

Giovanni, who had participated in a MSUD symposium in the United States, had links with an American support group for families dealing with MSUD. He had done a lot of research on MSUD and even designed a treatment protocol for his daughter, Laura, so he laid out the facts about MSUD for us.

"This disease is so difficult to treat because it can attack so viciously. A kid may be doing pretty well and seem healthy, and then all of a sudden, he/she gets very sick, and without skilled treatment, can die easily. In these MSUD crises, normal metabolism reverses itself and goes into catabolism. Catabolism refers to the destructive processes of chemical change characterized by the breaking down of complex substances into simpler ones and the release of lots of energy causing cells to be destroyed and turned into waste. Any kind of infection can result in a life-threatening situation. So, I do my best to protect Laura against this by giving her vitamins, avoiding contact with sick people, and, if we (the parents) are sick, we wear masks and wash our hands frequently when we're around her."

Then, Giovanni gave us the contact information for the most experienced doctors in the United States, Dr. Holmes Morton and Dr. Kevin Strauss from the Clinic for Special Children located in Lancaster County, Pennsylvania. Continuing his explanation, he said,

"This disease is so complicated and the doctors in Porto Alegre are the most experienced doctors in Brazil. And they are the only ones in Brazil with access to the proper equipment to read and monitor the levels of non-metabolized amino acids. You must seriously consider going to see Dr. Ricardo Pires."

I needed time to think…

I left Natal for Petrolina with a lot on my mind. Moving to Porte Alegre, a very distant city would be a huge financial burden. Driving would take at least three days, and flying was expensive, especially considering I would have to commute there regularly. So, if we did decide to transfer Artur there, I probably couldn't go with him, and this was breaking my heart.

My 16 hours sitting in a bus to Petrolina always gave me too much time to think. Should we take our son to Porto Alegre? How would I get enough money to pay for his expensive formula? Each container was about $500 and that only lasted for three days! I felt desperate and had to stop thinking about it and just move forward as best as I could.

I was in Petrolina when my biggest fear materialized. Soraya called saying that Artur had developed an infection and he was back in the hospital. I immediately got on an airplane to return to Natal.

We knew that MSUD adversely affects the patient's immune system, so infections are a major concern. Yslani was still in the ICU being treated for an infection and had not made any progress. This was so distressing for us, so we decided then and there that Artur would go to Porto Alegre as soon as he got rid of his infection.

After five days back in the hospital, the medications had cleared up Artur's infection and he was discharged. In the meantime, my brother-in-law, Arquimedes, had been taking the legal steps necessary that would allow Artur to go to Porto Alegre in the ICU airplane. His efforts were successful and we were preparing to leave.

Shortly before our departure, we got tragic news from the ICU nurse. "I'm sorry to have to tell you this, but Yslani just passed away. She had that infection and the doctors were treating it, but couldn't save her. We've never seen a situation quite like this; she was admitted with a single infection and, inexplicably, developed several more complications. She was too weak to fight."

Everybody was in shock. I tried to talk to her dad, Roberto, but he and his wife were sobbing inconsolably. And, what could I say to comfort them? What would people tell me if this had happened to Artur? My only option was crying with them.

I felt so bad for them. Yslani had had better care than Artur from the start, so, with her death, we felt even more vulnerable. Mr. Fernandes and Mr. Giovanni had told me that MSUD needs only a single illness or infection to cause a life-threatening crisis, and now, we also knew, even death.

I was now sure that going to another medical center would be the only chance for Artur. Even with all the efforts of the doctors in Natal, they were limited not only by their lack of experience with MSUD, but they also couldn't perform the critical task of screening amino acids levels in a timely manner. If these levels are not monitored frequently, they can quickly get out of control and lead to catastrophe. Under the circumstances, we were now convinced that going to Porto Alegre was our only option. We would continue to fight there.

CHAPTER 16

A VAIN ATTEMPT

We were approaching rock bottom

A knight may win a battle, but he knows that a war is bigger than that. He knows that he must always move forward, face several enemies and plan the strategy for the next battle. Artur, Sylvana and Soraya were on their way to Porto Alegre, but my mind was already thinking about a bigger step: the United States. I had already done the math: a treatment with American doctors (the best in the world), including food supplements, would cost approximately $6,500 per month.

I was planning to go back to Fortaleza to see my other son, Vinicius; however, I rushed from Natal to Petrolina when I heard that the former minister and senator, Dr. Jose Serra, was kicking off his presidential campaign in my city. I needed his help, so I had prepared a dossier describing my son's situation. I intended to personally hand it to Dr. Serra. My document included contact information for the MSUD doctors, directions for buying formula, and a story about Zachary Pinskey, an American kid born with MSUD, to show how effective the treatment in the United States was. According to his website, he was living a very normal life. My document was succinct and accurate. The only challenge was to reach out Dr. Serra.

It was not easy, but a congressman assisted me and put me face to face with Dr. Serra. Here was my chance. I explained to him about my son's case and gave him the documents I'd prepared. He seemed sympathetic and interested in helping my son, telling me he would try to help us get the care we needed. Dr. Serra asked the congressman's niece to oversee my case. Dr. Serra left our meeting to continue his busy campaign schedule while the congressman's niece remained briefly, telling me that Artur's case was a priority for her and her uncle and that she would move quickly toward a solution.

Brazilian politicians aren't known for quick responses, so I was really surprised when three days later, I received a call from an agent of the Brazilian Health Department. She told me that she had been assigned responsibility for Artur's case, adding that scheduling treatment in a foreign country with Brazilian government support would be very difficult to arrange. In other words, treatment in Brazil would be our only option. Despite that, I took this opportunity to question her about the MSUD formula, medicines and other costs related to his treatment. She couldn't answer my questions at the time, but agreed to study the case further and get back to me.

From this call, I was optimistic that a solution from the Brazilian government could be possible.

Days went by without any word from the health department. I began to feel that my efforts had failed. I was becoming frantic. The bills for Artur's treatment continued to pile up, and I had already exhausted all my personal funds to try to pay them.

Months went by without any further contact from our health department. Apparently, our case had fallen through the cracks of the Brazilian bureaucracy and now I was certain that my attempt was in vain. But I didn't give up. I pushed, called, insisted, and finally received a letter informing me that the government would provide formula for my son. *What great news!* However, the joy was short lived. They kept their promise in their own way; the supplement would be provided for only two weeks and nothing more.

I felt abandoned and like an idiot for having had so much hope. It was a vain attempt. Rock bottom was approaching with alarming speed.

Not wanting to waste more time, I talked to Arquimedes, my indispensable brother-in-law/lawyer, about filing a formal petition with the Health Department of Ceará State to request support for formula purchases and Artur's treatment in Brazil. We already knew that treatment in a foreign country could be easily denied.

CHAPTER 17

ROCK BOTTOM

What to do when you're caught in a trap?

I was desperate. I felt trapped with bankruptcy looming on the horizon. My family in Petrolina organized a fundraiser, which turned into a great event and gave me relief of two months. Friends organized campaigns; other organized raffles and I thanked everyone. This, however, was not the ultimate solution.

My family was thousands of miles apart. Vinicius was in Fortaleza with his grandmother; Soraya was with Artur in Porto Alegre, and I was in Petrolina. So, I had living expenses in each location to deal with in addition to buying formula for Artur. I needed to watch every penny I spent.

I needed to be creative, perhaps changing my work situation or even seeking a different job. I needed to live somewhere closer to my family. I looked for work in Fortaleza, but salaries weren't even close to what I was making in Petrolina. I couldn't begin to support my family on these salaries. So, in desperation, I decided to "bet all my chips," like a poker player going "all in," and start a new business. As an agricultural consultant and expert in designing irrigation systems, I wondered if I could open an irrigation company in Teresina-Piaui State, in a city relatively close to Fortaleza, where I could earn more money and also see my family more often.

I knew I couldn't afford any mistakes, so I spent a couple of months planning for this change. Even a small mistake could be fatal for my already struggling finances. I developed a business plan to present to a well-established irrigation company, a distributor from Israel. My proposal was for a partnership in which I would be their direct representative for the states of Piaui and Maranhao.

Gladly, they had agreed to support me with an advertising campaign, some display products, and they would pay for a grand opening party. It was a great deal for me; just having their logo on my store was a big plus.

But, for paying rent, buying shelves, office desks, computers, etc. I didn't have the money. So, with no other option, I sold my house to my brother, Ivaldo. Selling this house broke my heart, but I just closed my eyes and handed the keys to my brother. My dreams for my family included that house, but those dreams now had to change.

From this day on, I promised to myself not to think more about my house.

I still needed some financial support and my dad was more than willing to help. He gladly provided some furniture, shelves, and also some money. Even though he thought that my idea was crazy, he was very supportive. After months of preparation, I opened my company, Parnaiba Engenharia, in Teresina-PI. We were the only company in the region that could design irrigation projects and install them.

In Porto Alegre, Artur was finally gaining weight and his movements were improving. His seizures were gone and, after several days of treatment, he was discharged with orders that he should stay in Porto Alegre for further evaluation and follow-ups. A couple of months later, Soraya and my little king were back in Fortaleza.

My business was doing better than I had planned, and I could drive from Teresina to Fortaleza every Friday to see them. On Sundays, I would return to Teresina, a routine that lasted for over a year.

I had hit rock bottom and I was finally climbing out.

CHAPTER 18

THE GOOD SAMARITANS

Surrounded by friends, I sensed I could win the war

I dreamed of having my family back in Petrolina, but for now, it was not meant to be for the new generation of the Santos family. Due to Soraya's family support and a better medical center there, Fortaleza became our home city.

Back in Fortaleza, Soraya and Sylvana told me that Dr. Ricardo Pires and Dr. Renato were amazing. Beyond their MSUD knowledge, they were very supportive. Even though Dr. Pires was thousands of miles away in Porto Alegre, he continued as Artur's primary care physician. He had ordered a strict diet for Artur and recommended that he also have physical and occupational therapy to help him to improve his motor and cognitive skills. Most of these expensive therapies were not covered by our health insurance.

Artur was almost two years old now and his luck continued. His physical therapists were Drs. Eda and Sonia, two consummate professionals who treated Artur as their own. At first, most of the therapy sessions were done at home. We converted Artur's room into a little gym, so instead of toys, he had exercise apparatuses. MSUD had caused the left side of his body to be weak and underdeveloped. He also needed braces for both of his legs which he wore part of the time. Dr. Eda provided some of this equipment for free.

We hired a young nurse, Andrea, to help out at home. She was great with Artur and also provided a well-deserved break for Soraya. In only a few days, she became an expert on his complicated diet, lab schedules and medication. Artur definitely loved Andrea. If Soraya was out and he wasn't feeling well, he was always content to be in Andrea's arms. Soraya's unforgettable grandmother, Jasmina, generously paid Andrea's salary for us.

Artur's speech therapist, Dr. Isabela, was also amazing. She worked with him at least three times a week with her main objective being to relieve him of his feeding tube. When we finally took his tube out, feeding him by mouth became a real challenge. He had to be fed the special formula every three hours without fail or he would get sick very fast. Dealing with a baby who hadn't been eating normally and didn't want to eat took a lot of time and patience.

Artur's nutritionist was Dr. Soraya; her name was the same as my wife's. She was so kind. When we talked to her for the first time, she was quite honest in saying that she was unfamiliar with treating MSUD, but she would gladly do some research and work together with the doctors from Porto Alegre. In a few weeks, we became close friends.

Artur's pediatrician, Dr. Ariosto, was always available when we needed him. When Artur would become sick, Soraya would call Dr. Ariosto and he would often come to our house to treat him instead of having us take him to the hospital. My mother-in-law's friend, Dr. Ivaldo, was the same. Even though he was not a pediatrician, he came to check on Artur at least twice a week at no charge.

Even though we had not had a very easy life, we were somehow compensated by the friendships we developed with all of these good Samaritans. All of these people were amazing. They tried to do everything to help us.

Even though we had built a good supporting team, something was still hammering at my head. I was focused on going to the United States, where I was convinced that my son would get the care he needed. Sylvana, Soraya and Arquimedes felt the same. It was time to seek new Samaritans for my crusade. I was sure that, as more people got involved in this fight, the sooner we would overcome all barriers. Now, we already had many knights, but I would need to find more.

It was time to get back into the maze.

CHAPTER 19

SEEKING THE BEST

Each cell is a corral where eight amino acids jostle for space…

A strange corral

In 2003, Soraya and her sister, Sylvana, started communicating on-line with an American MSUD support group. Every two years, this group would host a symposium to discuss the disease and to exchange information with interested parties. However, our first opportunity to learn the reality about MSUD happened in Brazil when the Fernades family organized a small symposium in their home city of Natal. They had invited one of the USA's experts on MSUD, Dr. Kevin Strauss from the Clinic for Special Children.

I'll never forget Dr. Strauss' first lecture during which he emphasized the importance of knowing the consequences of MSUD when patients are not being treated properly. When MSUD is not properly treated, internal damage to cell systems will result in the destruction of the cells. To help us understand this type of crisis, he drew an analogy comparing a human cell to a corral and the essential amino acids to bulls that live in the corral. To be in balance, each corral (cell) has the capacity for eight bulls (amino acids). In other words, each cell requires eight amino acids to achieve the perfect cell balance. Hence, a perfect body with normal metabolism naturally maintains a normal balance of amino acids. Without this balance, the cell will be destroyed.

To help us visualize, Dr. Stauss drew an empty corral surrounded by the bulls, naming them for each of the amino acids essential to a human body: **Isoleucine**, **Leucine**, Lysine, Methionine, Phenylalanine, Threonine, Tryptophan and **Valine**. He then continued.

"I want all of you to consider that each bull has its own transporter, like a car, to get it into the corral."

Pointing to his drawing on the screen, he continued:

"This bull, called Leucine, is the strongest one and it has a very powerful transporter, like a brand new Ferrari. All the others have transporters like 1967 VW Beetles. And don't forget that the corral has a defect; it cannot get rid of the excess of three specific bulls, the Leucine, the Isoleucine and the Valine."

To finalize his comparison, he showed us the exact moment when a cell becomes toxic.

"It is logical that the Ferraris, with the Leucine bulls, will arrive at the corral first followed by the others. In normal cells, these amino acids are naturally metabolized and any excess is excreted through feces, urine and sweat, thereby keeping the cells in balance. But in the case of a cell with MSUD, all of the Leucine will enter the corral followed by Isoleucine and Valine as space permits. Some of the other bulls may be present in this corral, but as I said, **Leucine** is the fastest and the strongest and it will soon block the entrance for the others. The corral cannot support the pressure and eventually bursts. This is just what happens in the abnormal cells of an MSUD patient. The excess of these amino acids cannot be metabolized because of a defective enzyme and the affected cells are destroyed, causing a severe metabolic crisis for the patient. And to make it worse, this destruction occurs first and very aggressively in brain cells, which often can cause the death of an MSUD patient. Just a single infection, like a cold, can cause the cells' destruction, known as a catabolism, causing brain damage, and often death.

"Keeping an MSUD patient's amino acids balanced, especially Leucine, is a very difficult task. Close monitoring of the amino acid levels via blood tests is the only way to do it. When blood tests indicate that acid levels are not properly balanced, immediate action must be taken to prevent or mitigate a metabolic crisis. A special solution, called TPN, and some other drugs must be administered until the levels come back into balance…"

Even though we had done our own extensive research on MSUD, everything that Dr. Strauss had told us was completely new to me. I think I was stunned by his explanations and I found myself even more desperate to get answers to the many questions we had about Artur's condition. This symposium had become like a revelation for me; my eyes were finally opened. Dr. Strauss was the only doctor who provided a clear explanation about this terrible disease and that it could easily result in Artur becoming an invalid and even die.

I thought, "But could this doctor control the amounts of these amino acids (bulls) in each cell (corral)?" Later, I would find that these equations could not easily be balanced. According to Dr. Strauss, metabolism in humans is a rapid process with amino acid levels changing every second.

Dr. Strauss' presentation left us feeling like our treatment plan for Artur was severely lacking. In Brazil, we knew just two laboratories that could run the amino acids test, known as chromatography. One machine was in Porto Alegre and the other one in São Paulo. To make it worse, the laboratories had no interest in running these specific tests because the demand for them was very small. Also, to run the amino acid test, this multi-purpose equipment had to be reconfigured, a time-consuming process that delayed the results from 7 to 15 days. MSUD patients could not be treated effectively on such a lab schedule.

A patient could be dead in that amount of time! At Dr. Strauss' clinic in the USA, these lab tests would be available in about one hour, so any imbalance would be known and the patient could be treated right away.

During one of the symposium breaks, we had the opportunity to have a little chat with Dr. Strauss. When we told him how Brazil was treating its MSUD kids, he was surprised.

"It is impossible to effectively treat your patients on this basis. As I said, metabolism is a very fast process and cells react quickly and with great intensity. A fast turnaround by the lab is the only way we can know how to balance the cells, thereby avoiding a severe toxic situation and hospitalization."

I want to take my son to his clinic! This it was my only thought.

Since we had brought Artur's recent lab reports, including amino acid levels, X-rays, ultrasounds, etc., Dr. Strauss was able to do a considerably more complete review. Soraya had even pulled together photos showing the condition of Artur's body at various points in his young life. The doctor was simply amazed by the wealth of the material and asked if he could get a copy of it, which we provided. He told us that after the symposium, he would chart and analyze Artur's amino acid levels and provide us with a customized diet and feeding plan that would benefit him a lot. At the end of the day, he gave us a CD about a case of a malnourished Ethiopian child, pointing out that Artur's case was similar. He was suffering from malnutrition because we didn't have complete information to feed him properly. We would now have to prepare Artur's formula in a completely different way.

This symposium had opened a new chapter for us. We were now certain that we would have to seek better treatment for our son.

CHAPTER 20

THE UNITED STATES OF AMERICA?

A different world, where children with MSUD do not live in hospitals.

I was fighting in the wrong battlefield; the only tactic was to retreat and seek a new approach. This was how I felt after meeting with Dr. Strauss. Soraya and Sylvana spent days and nights at the computer communicating with people in the United States. They found that MSUD has a high rate of occurrence in Amish and Mennonite communities in the United States. These curious people live a simple, agrarian life, often apart from popular society and often without conveniences such as electricity, telephone, automobiles, etc. More than 400 cases of MSUD were logged in one such region.

Pointing at the computer screen, tearfully, Soraya showed me where Dr. Strauss' clinic was located. The setting for **The Clinic for Special Children** was in the heart of this beautiful Amish and Mennonite farming region where MSUD was so prevalent. Dr. Strauss was actually living among his patients. For us, this confirmed that he was our best hope. I now knew that our journey would take us to a distant American state with a strange sounding name, Pennsylvania, a place where I mistakenly thought the legendary Count Dracula was born.

Soraya's and Sylvana's persistence finally paid off. The MSUD Support Group that they had been in contact with asked us to be its guests at its symposium in Atlanta, Georgia, in June 2004. We were ecstatic, especially since the Support Group would also pay for our round-trip tickets and hotel. We briefly considered bringing Artur with us, thinking that we might arrange for him to see the American doctors, but dismissed this idea. Aside from being a long and stressful trip, no one from Dr. Strauss' clinic would be in attendance. Plus, we knew that Atlanta was a great distance from the clinic.

So, without even knowing a word in English, Soraya and I traveled for the first time to the United States of America to get more information about MSUD and to try to get advice on how to improve our son's treatment.

So far, we had not entered the new maze. Our frustration was about to begin.

Like everywhere, all foreign visitors arriving in the USA must pass through customs and be interviewed by an immigration officer. Just ahead of us in line, a young girl was crying, saying in clear Brazilian Portuguese, that she was denied entry. I felt sorry for her and thought that they must have their reasons for this kind of procedure. Now, it was our turn. The officer scrutinized our documents and asked some weird questions: Are you a terrorist? Are you bringing drugs with you? These questions seemed silly to us since we had already been interviewed back in Brazil when we submitted our application and paid the fee for our tourist visas. We could have either been approved or denied at that time. So, once we were granted our visas, I thought that everything was ok. I didn't realize that even my properly-issued visa did not guarantee that we would be admitted to the States.

The immigration officer questioned Soraya and I for nearly an hour. Our English was so bad that communication was nearly impossible. The officer was clearly frustrated so he called in an interpreter. To our great surprise and pleasure, the interpreter was from Recife, a Brazilian city near to Fortaleza. She was a lifesaver! During the interview, we continued to respond to the silly questions until we got trapped in one. The officer was questioning how we would be attending a symposium if we didn't understand the language. "Aren't the lectures in English?"

Wisely, Soraya asked me to give to our translator our U.S. contact information. I handed her a piece of paper with all MSUD Support-Group personnel information and the immigration officer called them. The officer talked to somebody from the MSUD Support Group. I assumed he spoke with Wayne Brubacher, husband of the MSUD

Support Group director Joyce Brubacher, and, just like that, all of our problems were gone. I didn't know what they told him, but our passports were immediately stamped with the typical six months' expiration. What a great relief!

As planned, volunteers from the MSUD Support Group met us in the baggage area and drove us to the hotel where the symposium would be held. Arriving at the hotel, we faced our second barrier with the language. Communication with the hotel clerk was not easy. However, she was courteous and gave me the keys while trying to explain something. I pretended to understand her and she pretended that everything was fine.

Finally settled into our room, my heartbeat went back to normal. Soraya and I rested a bit and then took a walk around the hotel. It was fantastic and, after a few hours wandering around the hotel and surrounding areas, we headed back toward the room, not wanting to get too tired. The symposium would begin the following day.

On our way back to the hotel, I began to realize why Brazil is considered a third world country. Although every country has its problems, the condition and cleanliness of the streets was not what it was here. They were immaculate. One thing that really caught my attention was a person buying a newspaper from a vending machine on the sidewalk. I had seen this in the movies, but I honestly was shocked. The man took a few coins out of his pocket, put them into the machine, and pulled a handle to open a little door to get the newspaper. What amazed me was, when he opened the door, he could have taken as many newspapers as he wanted, but only took one copy and walked away. As we stood nearby, this same scene was repeated, one person; one newspaper. *Such a system would fail in any Brazilian city. I'm sure the publisher would go bankrupt shortly.*

This was the first of many differences I would notice between Brazil and the USA.

We returned to the hotel exhausted from our sightseeing and slept until the next day. Early in the morning, we were starving and found that the hotel was serving the famous "American breakfast," Which is quite different from our breakfast, which is served with plenty of fresh juices, lots of fruits, strong aromatic coffee, a good variety of bread and cheese and our delicious "tapioca," a pancake made out of yucca which is commonly served in northeastern Brazil. In our first breakfast in the United States, they served a buffet with a huge variety of cereals, scrambled eggs, weak coffee, bacon, a dense, round wheat bread called a bagel, and some tasteless apples.

They also had pancakes served with a sweet, thick sauce. To our astonishment, this sauce was called maple syrup, the same as Artur's disease. Just smelling the syrup, I didn't have the courage to try it. It really reminded me of the smell in my son's room. But I tasted almost everything else.

With such a huge spread of food and portion sizes, it was very easy to understand why obesity in the USA is such a problem.

Everything was odd. The opening luncheon began at noon. Some of the attendees were dressed like cowboys that I've seen in western Bang-Bang movies. The women wore long dresses and a little bonnet. Later, we found out that they are members of a group of people with strong religious convictions and were part of the Mennonite sect. They basically make their livings on farms and the most conservative ones object to all worldly types of entertainment like TV, movies, sporting events, etc. A small fringe group of Mennonites can be confused with Amish people; they do not even use electricity or machinery in their daily lives. They seemed to be friendly people and even tried to communicate with us, but we had no idea how to respond properly. Our English was that bad. They probably thought that we were rude.

Joyce Brubacher, the MSUD Support Group director and symposium organizer, came to greet us. She spoke very slowly, but our conversation was cut short by our inability to understand clearly. Even so, I had prepared myself for this specific occasion, and in broken English, I thanked her for the opportunity that her group had given us. She introduced us to her husband and several other people from the group.

I was shocked when I saw the number of children playing in a room adjacent to the auditorium. Most of them were MSUD kids like Artur, but to my amazement, everyone seemed very healthy.

Seeing those children, I figured that our destiny was being laid out in front of us.

CHAPTER 21

DÉJÀ VU

In MSUD heaven

Before the symposium's grand opening, I wandered into the room where the MSUD children were playing. This area was a kid's paradise. There was a clown balloon artist; people applying fake tattoos, magicians, etc. The children loved it. We were curious about the bottle that the older children and adolescents carried with them, later finding out that they were carrying their MSUD formula in it. Everyone seemed very happy. I could only wonder if my Artur could be playing like them one day. He was now two years old and could barely move his body. Unlike these kids, we had to inject his formula into his mouth with a syringe. He hated this and I couldn't blame him. During the symposium, I tasted some other formulas and their flavors were quite different from Artur's, so I understood why these kids were taking their formula without much complaint.

One kid who was particularly enjoying this playroom stood out to me, like I somehow knew him from long ago or maybe I was just having a "déjà vu" experience. As he was about to get a Spiderman tattoo, I approached him and, in my very simple English, asked. "Are you Zachary?"

With a little suspicion in his voice, he replied, *"Yes."*

As soon as he answered positively, tears came to my eyes. It was him, Zachary Pinskey, the kid who I had read about on the website of the pharmaceutical company, Mead Johnson. His story inspired me because he was the only MSUD kid I had read about who was doing very well. His mother's postings on this website made me feel that it was possible to have happiness even with an MSUD son. I knew that Zachary had received the best care for his condition and, clearly, it had worked. My months of despair and all my feelings of failure were swept away like magic at this moment.

Just then, I realized that I might have been making a scene. Still in tears, I picked the boy up and hugged him as if I was hugging my own son. Just then, a very distinguished lady came over and said, "What's going on, Zach?" She introduced herself as Mrs. Denise Pinskey, Zach's mother. She was suspicious of me at first, and I couldn't blame her. After all, her son was with a stranger, but, somehow, she knew that we were the family from Brazil. She then took her son into her arms and the initial icy moments turned into a warm dialogue. Our interpreter had also just arrived and helped me to talk to the Pinskey family.

With the interpreter's help, I apologized for being so forward when I took Zachary into my arms and had her explain to them the reason for my delight at seeing him. We had a great conversation, me asking many questions and them telling everything about Zach's life and the problems that they had faced and continue to face. They were fantastic from the beginning to the end of our stay in Atlanta.

With this amazing experience, I imagined that one day my son would be playing just like Zachary.

At 1:00 pm, the symposium was about to begin. I struggled to understand what was going on and would occasionally pick up a word here and there. Thank God, a Portuguese lady was able to join us for a few hours. But when she had to leave, the speaker was in the middle of a lecture about nutrition. Soraya and I became like deaf people. We were completely lost.

Once again, we were very blessed. At the end of the day, Joyce Brubacher introduced us to an Argentine who worked for a computer company in the United States. Eduardo Gatica was the father of a MSUD child born in his home country. Fortunately, I could understand my new South American friend very well. Even though our native language is Portuguese, I had learned some Spanish through my business. The only thing we could not talk about was soccer, because soccer is almost like a religion in South America and should not be discussed, especially between Brazilians and Argentines if you are to remain friends.

On this basis, my friendship with Eduardo began. He told me the story about his daughter's MSUD and coming to the symposium on his own.

Mrs. Brubacher, the symposium host, joined Eduardo's and my conversation and told us a story about a case of MSUD in Brazil that reminded me of Yslani, the little Brazilian girl who died. Consequently, her story hit me like the sequel to a bad movie. With permission from the family, Mrs. Brubacher had published this story on the MSUD Support Group website.

Joyce Brubacher – Editor

"*I received a fax from Brazil on March 7 of this year. The urgent message was from João Carlos de Oliveira Mello, the father of a recently diagnosed infant with MSUD. His son, one month old, was undergoing dialysis in intensive care. He read on our Web site about TPN (Total Parenteral Nutrition) for MSUD, an IV solution available without leucine, isoleucine and valine that provides total nutrition via IV. It is now the recommended treatment for quickly lowering the branched chain amino acids (BCAAs). The baby was drinking the MSUD formula from Mead Johnson, but he wanted the TPN, which is more effective in reducing the high levels of the BCAAs. He wanted to know how to get it from the States as quickly as possible.*

"*João and I continued communicating by email. I sent information so his doctor could contact other experienced doctors both in the States and in Brazil. I also sent the information about where to get the BCAA-free TPN. On the 8th, Joao reported the baby was doing better each day. They were praying that their baby would soon be in good health again. They had followed instructions to get the IV solution.*

"Two weeks later, I realized I had not heard from him since the 8th. I sent an email asking how the baby was doing. His reply shocked us. The baby had died the week before. João said his son had died of complications from the MSUD. The MSUD TPN solution arrived too late because, as João says, 'The customs and bureaucracy here is unbelievable.'

"How very, very sad. João and his wife were married 12 years and this was their first child. Although the family had available resources to transfer the child to the U.S. for treatment, the health of the baby was too poor to permit transport.

"I asked João if I could tell about their experience in order to expose the plight of families in Brazil and other countries. He mentioned some of the medical problems they faced in Brazil. Only one laboratory in the country could provide BCAA levels in a short enough time to be useful for monitoring. And this was at a university far from their city. The medical food (formula) and TPN solutions have to be imported. In their situation, these were delayed in customs, and an extra charge of 88% was applied for the TPN (which is already very expensive)"…

The only difference between João's sad story and mine was that my Artur was still alive; but, listening to this story, I questioned myself "how is my Artur still alive?"

By the final day of the symposium, the Brubacher's, Eduardo Gatica, Nirmal Parmal and the Pinskeys were our best buddies. During breaks, we gathered to drink coffee and talk about our experiences. During one of our gatherings, we heard that one person had been cured of MSUD. At first, I guessed that I hadn't understood what was being said. But as I got confirmation that this had actually happened, I wanted to know more. So I grabbed Eduardo and went to meet the father of the girl who was freed of MSUD. He seemed suspicious, sometimes whispering as if he didn't want to be noticed. I didn't understand why he didn't want to talk much about it. So, Soraya and I decided that we should visit Dr. Strauss to get the full story, that is, if he would even agree to see us.

After the event, we thanked everybody especially Joyce Brubacher, who had helped us and then we prepared to leave Atlanta for our next destination, the state of Virginia. We were going to the home of Simone and Bruno, good friends of my sister-in-law Sylvana. Bruno, a very friendly Portuguese guy, told us to book our flight to Washington, DC, near their home, and that he would take us to Dr. Strauss' clinic, just a five-hour drive from his house.

From Virginia, our next destination would lead us to the rural farmlands of Pennsylvania.

CHAPTER 22

VACATION, WHO WOULD SAY THIS?

Time to breathe and to get ready for a new battle

Even a knight is entitled to a rest in the arms of his beloved lady. For over two years, Soraya and I had never had time to live as a couple. We were always dealing with Artur's health. When spending time with our new friends, we didn't know we could live as a normal couple with a chance to laugh, to travel, and to have fun. A disease like MSUD sickens an entire family. It is necessary to be very patient when facing such problems. Soraya and I went through several crises, but our love united us.

Arriving in Washington, DC, Soraya and I met Bruno for the first time at the airport. He told us that his wife, Simone, was at home preparing dinner and that she had sent him alone to pick us up. These were the only words he spoke during the 45-minute trip to his house. Obviously, Bruno was a man of few words. He emigrated from Portugal to the USA in his teen years and had been working in the construction industry since then.

During our very quiet ride to Bruno's house, we were delighted by the scenery. Everything was green and houses were becoming further and further apart. I had seen this only in Hollywood movies. At their house, Simone greeted us with great affection, like she had known us forever. She was one of the kindest, sweetest people that I had ever met. Her smooth voice was very calming to us, like music to our ears. Even though they were a young couple, it seemed as if they had realized "the American dream." Bruno was already a US citizen and Simone's Green Card was in process. Plus, they were living in wonderful place.

Before dinner, Soraya told the story about our struggle to keep Artur alive while Simone and Bruno listened, spellbound, in silence. Suddenly,

Simone started crying and asked what they could do to help us. Soraya told her that what they were already doing was more than enough and the trip to Dr. Strauss' clinic would be very difficult for us to make alone. Simone was not satisfied and pledged to help us with the costs at the clinic and our money would not be good during our stay here. Simone and Bruno would cover all these costs for us. Their generosity was overwhelming.

Soraya's sister, Sylvana, who knew Simone from an earlier visit to the US, told us that Simone's specialty is pasta with black olives, butter fried onions, garlic, and mayonnaise topped with grated parmesan cheese. Sylvana was right; it was so delicious that I barely could stop eating. During our dinner, time seemed to stop as Simone talked about Sylvana's and her adventures when they lived together in the USA. After this enjoyable meal, Bruno spoke a bit about his home country wineries and then excused himself and went to the living room to watch TV where he fell asleep. Without pausing, Soraya and Simone continued talking just like teenage girls. I was mesmerized by US TV and watched until bedtime. Our first night in our new friends' house could not have been better.

Our appointment with Dr. Strauss was in one week, so we spent the time as if on vacation, without a care. Simone and Bruno's hospitality was without limits; their house and their swimming pool were like our own. They took us to very nice restaurants and toured us around Washington, DC. The US capital interested me since I had read about Abraham Lincoln and I had a chance to see the house where he died and some wonderful museums.

Vacation was over!

When the day of our appointment arrived, we got up early, loaded into Bruno's brand new VW Passat, and drove to Strasburg, Pennsylvania.

With polished armor, sword in hand, a renewed spirit, the knight swiftly departed for a new battle.

CHAPTER 23

THE HOLY GRAIL?

My heart rate accelerated when I imagined that my Artur could be freed of MSUD

With equal parts of hope and doubt, we left Virginia and headed to southeastern Pennsylvania. As we approached Dr. Strauss' clinic, it seemed as though we were going back in time, like an old western movie. The modern worlds of Atlanta and Washington, now contrasted dramatically with a scene that I never imagined to exist in the U.S. Many people were dressed in very simple, dark-colored clothing, and instead of driving cars, they rode in black buggies pulled by horses. Throughout the area, beautiful farmland stretched for miles. Most farmers were working the land using equipment powered only by animals contrasting with others using modern farming equipment. The smell of manure was very intense. Some of the people working in the fields and driving buggies were dressed like those that we met at the symposium and some others with different clothing and long beards. As he drove, Bruno explained that those with long beards were Amish, a group of people belonging to a conservative religious sect. He knew little about them except that they live in groups, avoid modern technology like tractors, automobiles, telephones, etc. and stay pretty much to themselves. Bruno added that they were very well respected and admired for living in such a simple way. They seemed to be very friendly people.

Finding the clinic was not easy. We had seen the clinic on the Internet and knew that it was in a cornfield. We drove for some time, completely lost, until Bruno stopped a man in a passing buggy and asked for directions. The Amish guy explained how to get there and that we shouldn't be concerned about the small winding, largely abandoned, dirt roads...he assured us that we would arrive at the clinic.

I couldn't believe that I was there.

As we approached the beautiful wooden building that was the clinic, we all were taken aback. **The Clinic for Special Children** was, literally, in the middle of nowhere. As it turns out, this amazing place was built in the heart of Pennsylvania's Amish country because the occurrence of rare diseases among the Amish and Mennonite population there is the highest in the world. A local Amish family donated the land for the clinic and the community gathered to build it with its own hands. This local custom is often carried out when a family needs a new home or a new farm building and the community does the construction work, often in one day.

When Dr. Strauss arrived in the reception area and saw us, his jaw dropped in astonishment.

"My God, I didn't realize that it was you. Your friend, Nubia, talked to me and scheduled the appointment; so, I thought you were Brazilians who already lived here in America."

With a wide, welcoming smile on his face, he continued:

"Holy cow, you came all the way from Brazil just to see me? How's your boy? How long have you been here in the U.S.? Did you have to wait long for me? Do you miss Brazilian food...?"

He definitely had broken the ice and we began to be less anxious. We talked about Brazil and he told us that his trip there last year was the best of his life. Down to business, he explained that the Clinic for Special Children had quoted Nubia the normal consultation fee, thinking that the family was bringing a sick baby. In our case, the visit would be free of charge.

Are we still on vacation? I thought.

As Dr. Strauss led us to a conference room, he asked about the symposium, how we liked it; what was our plan to take care of Artur, etc. We really didn't have answers for him, so we just told him what he already knew, that Brazil was not even close to being able to offer the treatment that Artur needed. We were lucky that he was even alive. After contemplating our comments, Dr. Strauss spoke very slowly to allow Bruno to translate and described three treatment options for Artur.

"First, I could teach the Brazilian doctors the proper medical protocol for Artur; however, they aren't able to accurately and quickly check the amino acids levels. Plus, they have no place to purchase the TPN solution."

This was no good. Next! I thought.

"Second, you could come to live here, near my clinic, and I would work with Artur to stabilize his condition until we all were comfortable enough for you to return to Brazil."

Before my next thought, he laid out the third option.

"The third option, which I strongly recommend, is **to cure Artur's MSUD**."

When he told us our third option, we were speechless. We had heard very little about the cure during the symposium in Atlanta. Soraya and I started to cry. Bruno and Simone couldn't hold their tears, and neither could Dr. Strauss. Could our prayers be finally answered? My heart rate skyrocketed as I pictured Artur, cured and playing with his brother. We all needed a break to compose ourselves.

Shortly thereafter, Dr. Strauss continued,

"The cure for MSUD is a special liver transplant using a specific protocol we developed here in cooperation with Children's Hospital of Pittsburgh."

Turning his attention to Soraya, he continued,

"And you, Mom, after this transplant, you will be able to get rid of all MSUD formulas, apparatus, etc. Your son will be able to eat everything."

A miracle? No more formula? Have we found the Grail? I thought.

These sweet words from the American doctor were sounding like the best melody and lyrics I had ever heard.

"This protocol is new with fewer than 10 patients treated thus far, but in every case, the patient has been cured of MSUD and is living a near-normal life. We have been studying these patients after transplantation and know that their cognitive ability is amazingly high when compared to other MSUD kids who haven't had transplants. And most importantly, every patient's amino acids levels have come into balance immediately after the transplant. The waiting list for MSUD transplantation is growing very fast though. For the problems that you face and from where you come, I'm sure this is the best option. You cannot imagine how different the life of a child becomes when he can eat regular food. We've had children who ate a hamburger five days after surgery."

He then turned directly to Soraya. *"Do you want your son cured? I just want to know if you want to see your child living well."*

Her voice trembling and tears flowing she said, "yes" without hesitation. Despite that, he oddly asked her the same question again and then again, at least three more times. Each time he asked, she responded emphatically "yes," "yes," "yes." Then, to provide an outlet for this emotional apex, Dr. Strauss laughed and admitted that he actually understood Portuguese. Soraya's responses needed no translation. His little joke melted the stress in that room and our laughter could be heard throughout the clinic.

As soon as I regained my composure, my mind filled with questions and I did not keep them to myself. I spit them out barely giving enough time for translation. "How much would the surgery cost? Could it be done in Brazil? Would Dr. Strauss help us to deal with the U.S. immigration system?" I told him that September 11 had complicated the visa process a lot. Instead of answering these concerns, he called in his colleague, Dr. Holmes Morton. Just like Dr. Strauss, he spoke in a gentle way.

"Even though the protocol was developed between our clinic and Children's Hospital of Pittsburgh (Children's), Children's is the one that does the surgery and, of course, quotes the cost in advance to the patient's family. Although the clinic is involved with the transplant, there is no additional charge for our efforts."

He then excused himself from our meeting to call Children's to ask for an estimated cost. As he walked away, I questioned myself – how this could be possible? I was in front of the two biggest MSUD experts in the entire world and even though they didn't know us well they were treating us with such generosity that was impossible to summarize their solidarity.

I was mesmerized!

Meanwhile, Dr. Strauss explained the procedure in some detail, making sure that we were aware of the risks involved with such an operation. Children's had had a success rate of over 99% for liver transplantation in non-MSUD cases and 100% for MSUD cases. Brazil's success rate for liver transplantation was far from these numbers. In other words, a high percentage of transplants in Brazil failed and the patients died. Based on this record, he ruled out the option of having the surgery done in Brazil for several reasons: Brazil's death rate was high, the Brazilian medical establishment had no protocol established, nor did it have the necessary equipment for liver transplantation for MSUD patients. Without the protocol and equipment, not to mention the experience, the risks would be immeasurable. Plus, the waiting list for livers in Brazil was so long that it would take at least 4 to 5 years to get a suitable donor for Artur. In the United States, however, a MSUD patient goes immediately to the top of the list because in the USA, MSUD is considered a high-risk disease.

Dr. Morton returned and told us that the procedure was, not surprisingly, very expensive. Children's estimated the cost at $250,000. Without hesitation, I said. "Okay, imagine that I can get this money in a few months. Will you help us with paperwork and will your clinic monitor our case?"

Soraya had no idea where I was coming from, so very angrily she whispered to me in Portuguese. "Where are you going to get that money? Are you going to rob a bank? Are you crazy…?"

My brain was working so fast that I couldn't answer her and I didn't want to waste the doctors' time. So, I just asked her to stay calm and that I'd tell her about my plan later.

Dr. Strauss offered to provide us a letter to support our visa application and that he would gladly consult with Children's to assure that Artur would get the best possible treatment.

Our meeting ended with the understanding that we'd meet again as soon as possible. In the meantime Dr. Strauss would look into helping us finance the operation with resources that might be available in the USA and that I would look into it in Brazil. We thanked them and began our trip back to Virginia.

When I got into Bruno's car, Soraya was furious with me. "You're a lunatic. Tell me, where are you going to get this money? Do you have another life that I don't know? Where? Tell me where the money is coming from. I want to know right now!"

I understood her reaction. She was very emotional and was thinking only about Artur. She was unable to figure out that we had a real chance to get the money. Actually, simple math could solve our problem. So, I cut her off.

"Just relax and let me explain. You know that Brazil is now paying for Artur's formula, right? And it costs around US$60,000 a year. Are you following me?"

"Yes, go ahead!"

"If Artur lives for ten years with MSUD, the Brazilian government will be paying US$600,000. So, for the amount related to only about four years' supply of formula, we can get the cure and the Brazilian government's obligation to us will be eliminated. This obligation could even be much higher than US$600,000 depending on Artur's life span. We can prove that the transplant will save money since it will cure the MSUD and eliminate any future government involvement. We just need to convince the government to cover the cost of the cure."

At this, Soraya calmed down, and apologized for her outburst.

Now, inside another maze, we had to find our way out.

CHAPTER 24

BAGS FULL OF HOPE

The fight will be between two lions

Have our prayers finally been answered?

For months, I had been dreaming of having my family back, buying a new house, and starting a new life. Even with the financial problems and emotional despair that we were facing, I felt I could see that the light at the end of the tunnel was growing brighter. I could picture Vinicius playing in my front yard and Artur eating anything he wanted. I could see Soraya smiling again and our house full of friends, just like it was in the past.

How could we convince the Brazilian government to pay for Artur's special liver transplant?

Our first business upon returning home would be to meet with Soraya's lawyer brother, Arquimedes, and explain to him how we planned to get the Brazilian government to support us for Artur's liver transplant. I knew that by law, the government must provide support for treatment of medical conditions that cannot be effectively treated by the Brazilian medical system. So, during the flight, Soraya and I brainstormed for hours. Our goal was to have Arquimedes file a claim against the Brazilian government for the financial support that the law guarantees its citizens, but which you often must fight for. I figured that our primary arguments would be:

> 1st - The oldest Brazilian MSUD victim was diagnosed too late and he was now 15 years old, still unable to eat normally and dependent on the government for assistance. With Artur's earlier diagnosis and improved treatment methods, he could easily live longer than that; let's say 30 years. So, at current prices for

formula and other essential services, he would cost Brazil more than US$5 million.

2nd - At least 10 MSUD cases had been identified in Brazil, so they could also benefit from our action. Curing those kids would be a great opportunity for Brazil to improve its MSUD treatment capabilities and save money at the same time.

With these arguments, especially the fact that the government could save a great deal of money, I had no doubt that we could convince the authorities to support us, thereby solving our problem of how to pay for the transplant. I was thinking we could move very quickly with the surgery. And according to Dr. Strauss, a couple of days after surgery, Artur would be discharged. He'd then have a period of recovery and we would be back in Brazil in six months or less. The wheels were turning now and I was beginning to count the days until my little king was cured.

Where is the maze?

At home, I summarized the math that made my argument valid. However, as an attorney, Arquimedes' skeptical eyes had a different view. He asked a few questions and told us that he would have to think about it. I added that Dr. Strauss would support us in any way we needed to strengthen our petition to the government. Arquimedes thought that our arguments seemed solid, but added:

"Convincing the federal lawyers will be difficult. They will see us only as numbers, not as humans. Give me a few days to come up with a strategy."

Arquimedes was the perfect partner for me as we made our case for government support. Where I was the bull in the china shop throwing ideas out right and left, he moved ahead in a slower, more contemplative way, carefully thinking through everything and occasionally reining me in as I tried to stretch too far and too fast. Unlike me, he almost never acts on impulse. Even though he was a very young lawyer, I had great confidence in him. I knew that he wouldn't move a step without being certain that we would achieve our goal. Soraya and I wanted to start the process immediately, but Arquimedes methodically thought everything through in order to develop the best possible case.

His total dedication to his nephew's case was obvious; he just wanted to get it right the first time. He knew that our argument must be flawless, saying:

-"Our argument must be well-conceived and thoughtfully presented to get the judge's attention and support. I agree that the cure is the best outcome for Artur and for the state. Idario's math proves it, not to mention that it is his constitutional right. However, we must be prepared for anything when it comes to the feds. Their objective will be to defeat us in any way possible, despite the logic of our arguments. And even if we win the case, it's likely that they'll appeal. So just be prepared for a nasty, and possibly long fight. Getting this financial support, especially since the money will be going into the U.S. medical system, this will be very difficult."

This invisible wall is not going to stop me. Will it? Am I a knight or a peasant?

The documents we needed from Dr. Strauss and Children's Hospital were very easy to get; however, to get the Brazilian doctors to endorse our plan was a different story. Soraya begged these doctors to provide a letter of support. But they claimed that they could not provide such a document because they didn't know enough about this special procedure to support it. Since these letters were proving so hard to come by, I pushed Arquimedes to abandon them and present our case only with Dr. Strauss' letter, but he wouldn't have it.

"Documents from the US won't be enough. Without letters from our own medical professionals, it will be easy for the feds to argue that the Americans just want the money. The feds will destroy our case on our first attempt. We cannot take that risk."

Where are the good Samaritans?

Once again, Soraya begged Dr. Ricardo Pires to endorse Dr. Strauss' protocol. Dr. Pires was the one who confessed that providing such a statement would put his position at risk.

"Soraya, do you have any idea what you are putting me through? My boss will come after me with no mercy. I'll get in touch with Dr. Strauss and I will do what is right for your son. Give me a couple of days and you'll get your letter."

For a moment, Soraya was speechless at Dr. Pires' words. Now, at least we had one supporter. Later, we got letters from Dr. Carla Soraya and Dr. Ivaldo.

After almost two months of collecting the necessary documentation, Arquimedes had finally pulled the pieces of this "puzzle" together. His next step was to present the case to the state's public defender to determine if they would represent us against the government. If they accepted it would then be a "fight" between two Brazilian governmental institutions, giving our side added strength and validity. Arquimedes stressed, "If I file this petition by myself, it would be like a lion (the government) fighting against a rabbit (Artur). But if the public defenders agree to accept our case after reviewing our documentation, then we can consider ourselves on equal grounds."

Soraya and I had total confidence in Arquimedes' skills as a lawyer, and, knowing that his love for his nephew was driving him throughout this process, I never considered getting a second opinion. He knew Artur's life was at stake and my only concern was our opponent in this battlefield, the Brazilian legal system.

CHAPTER 25

VICTORY!

The celebrations did not last; we had to stomach some devastating defeats

Not surprisingly, Arquimedes' tactic was successful when he convinced the public defenders to accept the case. This was Artur's first victory. In the meantime, with Dr. Strauss' intervention, Children's Hospital of Pittsburgh reduced the price of the surgery to $90,000. On top of that, an American foundation that Strauss had worked with in the past, agreed to provide $25,000, effectively reducing the amount of financial support needed from the Brazilian government from $225,000 to only $65,000. This amount represented only a little more than one year of formula. The petition was revised on this basis and resubmitted to the court.

Finally a victory!

The judge gave the Brazilian Health Department two months to comment on our petition. We weren't surprised when their reply came only two days before the two-month deadline and they decided that the Brazilians doctors would examine Artur, and, based on their findings, the health department would make a final determination.

For us, this was fair, so we agreed. The judge set the date and the place to proceed with the case.

The day for the appointment with the judge arrived, and to my dismay, I couldn't attend. I was being pulled in all directions, especially with my job. I, therefore, reluctantly accepted Arquimedes' advice that he and Soraya could handle the meeting. After all, he had become an expert on all aspects of our case. The hearing was very tense. A physician from "Hospital das Clinicas" of Sao Paulo, persuaded by the feds, told the judge that taking our boy to the United States for his care was stupid, adding that she could do the transplant blindfolded! We had checked her credentials before the meeting and knew that she didn't have any experience treating MSUD and perhaps hadn't even heard of it before this case, but she declared that Artur looked very good and she was sure that he could wait until the Brazilian medical establishment was qualified to treat and cure it.

Arquimedes explained that Brazil had no protocol for liver transplantation in MSUD cases, adding that we didn't have a machine available to check amino acids levels nor did we have access to TPN solution or the capability to handle it. When we insisted that Artur could not wait between four and six years, the normal time on Brazil's waiting list, the federal lawyer cut in, saying it was all nonsense to spend such amount of money, suggesting that, with this money, Brazil could buy a machine and send a doctor to the United States to learn how to use it. This is when Soraya exploded at the federal lawyer.

"You will not use my son as a guinea pig! This doctor has absolutely no experience with MSUD and she dares to declare that my son can wait! With the speed that things happen here in Brazil, my son will be in a wheelchair or in a grave by the time this machine is available and the protocol has been adopted here. What would you do if it were your son?"

Even more furious now and aiming to prove that the Brazilian doctor had no MSUD experience, she turns to her. "Have you ever treated anyone with this disease? How many liver transplants have you done for MSUD patients? Do you even know about the protocol?"

The doctor didn't respond to Soraya's verbal attack before the federal lawyer intervened and turned to the judge to insist that sending Artur to the United States would cost Brazil a fortune and set a precedent for other families who have children with MSUD.

With this stupid argument, the hospital room went silent for a minute or so. The judge, speaking for the first time in these proceedings, stopped this obviously inexperienced attorney and demanded.

"Wait a minute! So, what are we discussing here? Is it about money or is it about the life of a child? You obviously don't know that our constitution guarantees appropriate medical care for our citizens. Not only that, but you either didn't read or perhaps misunderstood the petition, but Brazil is not spending money, but saving money. Did you understand that? If money is the issue and this kid's life is not, I will end this hearing now. You should wait for my verdict."

Victory!

The court ruled more quickly than we could have imagined, determining that the federal government, the state of Ceará, and the City of Fortaleza should confirm the expenses of sending Artur to the United States for treatment. This ruling was clearly a win for us and we were overjoyed. However, in Brazil, a judicial decision can be appealed and it was; the appeal resulted in the revocation of the judge's decision. Dejected again, we had to start over. Arquimedes explained:

"Our case can be appealed over and over, even to our Supreme Court. We can keep winning at each level, but it will take so long for this process that we may lose the chance to help Artur."

The appeal was directed to the Regional Court in Recife, the capital of the state of Pernambuco. Just as before, we won the right for treatment in the USA. And again, we were very happy. But, as Arquimedes had warned, the feds appealed the decision again. Only this time, the federal lawyers filed an appeal for total dismissal.

The President of the Regional Court ruled in favor of Brazil, and we lost the right to have our son treated in the United States.

"Brazil's Injustice" had ended our dreams for Artur. Are we totally defeated?

Arquimedes went immediately to talk to the public defenders. They explained that it would be very difficult if not impossible to reverse this decision. All 12 judges of this court would have to render an opinion and it would be unlikely that they would go against the President. Bottom line: they said that it was a waste of time for us to appeal. Arquimedes returned home with the bad news, prompting Soraya to tell him to take her to the public defender lawyers. She wanted to speak to them directly. There, in tears, Soraya was very persuasive and convinced our defenders to fight for her son. For us, this would be Artur's last chance.

On the day of the next hearing, Arquimedes thought he should go to Recife and try to talk directly to the President Judge since he would be presenting the case to his 11 colleagues. We had no assurance that we'd even be able to reach this judge, although it couldn't hurt to try. After all, this was our final chance.

Arquimedes' trip was worth it because the judge's secretary gave him five minutes with the judge. Facing the 5th Regional Court President, Arquimedes pointed out that the feds' appeal had failed to include the fact that the cost of the transplant surgery had fallen from $250,000 to $65,000. So, the government's financial exposure was significantly less. Having made his five-minute appeal to the judge, Arquimedes waited for the results of the vote, which came at the end of the day.

Unbelievably, we had succeeded. He grabbed a phone and screamed to Soraya.

"They voted unanimously in our favor, all 12 of them! We've defeated the system. Yee-ha! You can celebrate now."

Victory!

So far, our battle had cost us more than eight precious months, but now we figured that we could make our plans to go to the United States. However, when Arquimedes got back to Fortaleza, we had another reality check; the decision could still be appealed to the Supreme Court.

"If this happens, the bureaucratic red tape could take years and the chances are slight that the lower court ruling would be upheld. In most cases, the Supreme Court favors Brazil. The case is supposed to be returned to Fortaleza's court to be expedited. I'll push them to move faster so we can avoid another appeal from the feds."

Days later, the worst possible thing happened. The ruling in our favor would not be upheld. The feds had initiated an appeal to the Supreme Court. And trying to talk to the President of the Supreme Court was like trying to talk to the President of Brazil, an impossible mission. We knew of no one who could intervene on our behalf. The process would take years.

Victory from "Brazil's injustice." They had ended our dreams for Artur.

CHAPTER 26
PERSISTENCE TRIUMPHS
For each yes, there was a no

The knight and his lady were fading. The maze became increasingly more complex. With this last defeat, Soraya sank into a deep depression. It seemed to her that all hope was gone. About this same time, matters became worse when Artur went into an MSUD-generated crisis, falling into a coma and almost losing his vision. Thank God, he came out of it.

Finally, after several months of anguish, the Supreme Court ruled in our favor with the judge, Nelson Jobin, ordering that support from the Brazilian government be expedited. The feds could not appeal anymore. The prosecutor informed us that, in a few days, we would have the necessary paperwork to proceed with the medical treatment plan in the United States.

Now it's for real, VICTORY! I fully credit Arquimedes with this positive outcome. His untiring efforts will never be forgotten.

On the day of this ruling, I was working in Teresina when Soraya told me the good news. *"Get ready. We'll be going to the United States soon."* At this, I jumped into my car and drove to Fortaleza to be with my family and begin to make preparations to leave.

In less than two weeks, I had to have everything organized. I considered turning my business over to my employees to run. However, I knew things could easily go downhill without my supervision. So, I decided just to close it and restart when I returned. Besides, I needed money to prove to the American consul that I could afford to support my family in the United States. Selling my business inventory would generate some cash for this purpose.

Excited, we went to the American embassy in Recife to get a visa for Artur. Our plans were for Soraya and I to take Artur to the United States and Vinicius would stay in Brazil with his grandmother, Gardenia. Then, once we were settled in the US, I'd return to Brazil while Soraya and Artur waited for the transplant. I'd return to the US for the transplant and recovery period and then, we'd all go home to Brazil.

That was our plan!

At the American embassy, we met with the Consul who, surprisingly, spoke Portuguese very well. We explained why we were there. He said he understood our need, but threw us another roadblock.

"I see that the Brazilian government has approved your case, but I need to have proof that the financial resources have been sent to the United States and that you also have the means to support your family in the States. This is not a denial of your application. Just have the funds wired to the United States, show me the documentation, and I'll issue the visas.

We headed back to Fortaleza to provide what was requested. While on our way back, at 'out of the blue', changing what we had planned, Soraya made a good point. *"All four of us must go to the States as a family. I won't live alone in a strange country with a sick child, knowing nobody and not speaking the language. So, prepare yourself to come and stay for the duration…Vinicius will come with us as well. It doesn't make sense for Artur and me to be in the States, you in Teresina, and Vinicius in Fortaleza.* **We must go as a family.***"*

When the money was transferred to the US, Soraya and I went back to the American embassy in Recife to finally get our family visas. After arriving there very early in the morning, we finally had our interview about 4 p.m. I couldn't believe that we had had such treatment. Nobody came to talk to us for the entire day. Finally, the consul came out and told us that he believed that the money was wired, but he couldn't talk to anyone in the United States who could prove that the money had actually been transferred. The American Consul told us that nobody at Children's Hospital could confirm that the money had arrived. Soraya showed the document proving that she had transferred the money and she suggested that he should talk with Dr. Strauss. He was the one who had guided us on the wire transferring process. Dr. Strauss explained to him that he would not find the money at Children's Hospital, because it had been wired to the AJS Foundation for Msd in Philadelphia, PA. The consul then called the Foundation and confirmed the transaction.

With everything resolved, we were told that we should expect our visa stamped passports by mail.

They arrived! All four passports each stamped with a tourist visa and permission for multiple entrances for a period of five years.

We were about to reach the Grail

Here we go to the United States!

CHAPTER 27

FAREWELLS

I had to leave without looking back

Saying goodbye to my family in Petrolina was my next challenge. All my brothers and sisters were waiting for me. I was very emotional; my mother consoled me. At the kitchen table, I gathered myself together and explained to everyone about our plan to go to the United States. My father gave me a big hug and told me that he could not imagine how I was handling such pressure. He then offered me more money and asked me to keep him informed of everything. He didn't want to see my family struggling in a foreign country. My mother added,

"My son, from the bottom of my heart, I would like you to stay here, but I know that what you're doing will be good for your child. What is good for your son will be good for you. Don't worry. Wherever you are, my heart and my thoughts will be always with you. On your journey, every time that you face trouble, do not forget that the Lord is at your side. Be strong. I have faith that God will calm the violent waters and you will be blessed."

She paused, sobbing, and then continued.

"You know that you can always count on your family. Rest assured that God chose you for this mission because He thinks you're capable of it. Remember that He will never abandon you. My heart is aching, but, at the same time, it is full of joy because of what you have achieved. You are clearly my most fearless son. May the peace of God be always with you..."

Then, she kissed me and went to her room crying. My siblings hugged me and we cried together. Each one offered me words of support and affection. Even my father was speechless. When I settled down, I wanted to see my grandfather, Sebastião.

I didn't realize it at the time, but I was about to face the toughest part of my farewell. Grandpa Sebastião was over 90 years old, still working, and still had a clear mind. He came to my father's house; we both sat on the sidewalk and, in his normally funny way, he started the conversation.

"Are you really going to cross the big lake (he meant the ocean)?"

"Yes, I will, Grandpa. Artur will be healed there."

"Are you sure that 'galeguinho' (this was his name for Artur – he meant little blond kid) will be cured?"

I nodded and in simple words I tried to explain why he needed to go to the United States. He then said,

"I know you're fearless. I admire you; nobody can stop you. I also never imagined myself here in Petrolina. I was born in Prata and it looks like that I'll be buried here. I just have to tell you that you must leave to save your son, but be sure of one thing; we will not see each other again. This will be our last goodbye."

Again, I was in tears. His words pierced my heart as if I had been punctured by a gigantic arrow. He meant that I was leaving to save a young life, but would be losing an old one. He was predicting that he would die in a short time. He didn't mean to hurt me. I knew his intentions, but I was not expecting to hear that. I told him that I would prove him wrong.

"Grandpa, don't say such a thing. You're healthier than me! In a few months, I'll be eating beans with you in your house. It won't take that long to have our 'galeguinho' back playing with you."

He hugged me, gave me a blessing and sent his best regards to the rest of the family. After he left, I went inside to my parents' house and asked my dad if grandpa was sick. My dad said that he was fine. I guessed this old man was just facing reality.

When my siblings left, I spent a few more hours with my mother and father talking about Artur and my plans to return to Brazil as soon as possible. My father told me that on my return, he would help me to restart my business.

Once again, I had to alter my dreams and forget about my promising business. My brother, Ildeci, was in charge of closing my company. I left him some money and my pickup truck in case he needed them. The bureaucratic red tape involved with closing a company in Brazil is excessively complicated and time-consuming. I still feel indebted to my brother for this gigantic favor. In Fortaleza, I had to break my apartment lease, pay all pending bills, and give away my furniture and household items. The Ford Fiesta that was originally my wife's was now Arquimedes', not as a payment, but as a reward for his hard work.

It is amazing how life turns around. Not long before, some people likely envied the lifestyle of my young family. We had our own house, two cars, a pick-up truck, a motorcycle, a maid, a nanny, our first child, a farm, our own company, prestige and many friends. For a young couple in Brazil, this is a dream that few can achieve. I was proud of my career as an agronomist. Even though I was very young, I knew I was a respected engineer in my area and I was contributing to my country's development. With all this, I felt lucky.

When Artur was born, my life was turned upside down. Now, I was leaving everything in my world behind to live, temporarily, I thought, in different world.

Despite the sadness of departing from everything and everyone that I knew, I was happy. Every minute, I was getting closer to what was really important: the cure for our king. My grail.

CHAPTER 28

BACK IN THE USA

At three years of age, Artur was on a path toward the "Grail"

I have not spoken so often about them in these last chapters, but our good Samaritans continued to give us hope. As our departure neared, we were terrified. The language barrier was our main concern, but there were more questions unanswered. How do we book a hotel there? Would it be better to rent a house? Will we need a car?

A phone call days before our departure gave us some peace.

"Hi, Soraya. How are you doing? It's Simone calling from United States!"

"Hi, Simone. We are fine. How is Bruno? Sylvana is here; I'll get her."

"Bruno is OK. No, don't get Sylvana. I want to talk to you. Bruno and I want you and your family to stay with us when you come to the States. You guys can stay here as long as you need. Pittsburgh is not too far from here and we'll find a way to arrange transportation and help you in any other ways that we can."

For sure, Simone and Bruno's offer ended a lot of our concerns about the trip.

We're leaving to face a new life. God, please protect us, and give us a better life than what we have now.

While waiting at the airport in São Paulo, Vinicius was blowing bubbles in his drink with a plastic straw. Artur began laughing; the very first time we had ever seen this. He laughed so loudly that I had to ask Vinicius to stop in case this was bothering the others. Soraya saw this differently.

"They are just kids. Don't worry; everything is fine."

Regardless, this was what Artur needed. He was smiling; his family was together; his brother could bring joy to his life. Artur really hated taking his formula and he cried every time we fed him. So, this laughter was really what he needed to somehow offset all the bad times. We were so hopeful.

Finally on the plane to the United States, we didn't know how Artur might react to such a long flight. And we quickly found out why such long trips are so tough for any kid, let alone a kid with MSUD. On the plane, Artur refused to take his formula and our normal tactics to force him to eat at home didn't work. But, we knew he had to eat. So in our first attempt, he ate about 20% of what he needed. Three hours later, we tried again and he ate nothing and became even crankier. We tried to calm him down in every way, until he finally fell asleep, exhausted. Soraya's concern persisted.

"If he doesn't eat, he will have an MSUD crisis. As soon as we get there, you better feed him."

"Relax, I promise that as soon as we check in with customs, I'll feed him."

A long trip to the U.S. with an MSUD kid was a problem. But, going through immigration services was a nightmare. We were detained for several hours while the officials were inspecting the cans of formula. They asked me some questions, but I didn't understand. I was so nervous, and the only thing that I could say was: *"Water – water."*

I was desperate for water to prepare my son's formula. We had to feed Artur and I couldn't explain this to them. All the while, Artur was getting worse, crying so loud the officer became annoyed. I handed a letter to the officer from Dr. Strauss about the formula, telling what it was and why it is needed. He glanced at it and asked us to hold on for a moment. They already had opened one can and they were about to open more. So, I yelled **no!, no!, no!...** I wanted to say more, but didn't know how to say. My concern was that the formula would become contaminated and therefore useless. As these officials talked, I heard them say "ANTHRAX." This was one of the few words that I could understand. At the time, I knew that anthrax was in the news in the United States. So, when they mentioned it, I was adamant. "No Anthrax. No Anthrax."

But as much as I tried, I couldn't get them to understand me. Then, the situation became even more intense. They brought in dogs to smell our bags and boxes. By this time, Artur was out of control. I asked for a translator and they finally found a police officer who spoke to me in Spanish. I felt relieved, I knew Spanish, so I told him what was going on.

"My son suffers from a rare disease called MSUD. He needs to take his formula or we could face a medical crisis."

This police officer was very sympathetic and he asked me to calm down. He spoke to the immigration officials and, immediately, Soraya was permitted to feed Artur. The police officer brought us a sealed water bottle. I thanked him and tried to pay him back for the water. He refused my money and again, told me to stay calm.

At that point, I didn't know what was happening. I don't know if they called Dr. Strauss or not, but they finally allowed us to pass through customs.

We collected our baggage only to find everything had been opened and was totally messed up. The boxes containing the cans of formula were destroyed. We threw away the two cans of formula that they had opened. At least, Artur had, at that point, been fed and he and Vinicius were doing OK. As I struggled to get our stuff out of the baggage claim area, one of the officers brought me two carts and a roll of duct tape. This really helped a lot.

Finally, we were officially in the USA. *At three years of age, Artur was on his way to be freed from MSUD.*

CHAPTER 29

THE WINDOW'S MOTOR?

King Artur and his knight, Sir Papa, could get it all.

Putting aside our endless problems, we had many hours of joy with Bruno and Simone. I felt like we had left our problems in Brazil. Having my family together under the same roof, even if it wasn't our own house, renewed my spirit. I was so tired. Three stressful years had passed where, because of my job, I could only see my family twice a month. And during these visits, I was dealing only with problems. During these days with our friends, the past had become just a memory and the future was so blurry we couldn't focus on any specific plan. So, we settled into a comfortable routine, enjoying our time together and living like a family. Despite not having a playmate his age, Vinicius seemed content. Artur was calmer in this new environment. And the best thing of all was that Soraya was laughing again.

Family life is without a doubt the most important way of learning. It is like living next to God, celebrating new experiences, setting goals, and, most importantly, giving back to our children and friends what our parents gave to us. At Bruno's house, I could laugh with my kids. I could talk with my wife about things that were not related to problems, and I could spend as much time as I wanted with them. I realized that Artur needed my support much more that I thought. Here, I could be part of their lives. We could sort of start over; I could think straight.

Bruno was mature beyond his age. He advised me that I should look for a job. I went to see his workplace a couple of times. We had a meeting with his boss, Carlos, who told me that the doors were open for me whenever I was ready. I had no legal papers to work with him, but his generous offer made me feel good. Simone took me to consult a lawyer about changing my visa status. I appreciated these efforts and learned from them, but I only had two thoughts: to have Artur cured and then to return to my life in Brazil.

Despite the comfort we had with our friends, one problem could not go away. Except for an occasional French fry or a spoonful of rice (very low protein food), Artur's only nourishment was his formula. Eating almost anything else could throw him into a metabolic crisis and a trip to the emergency room. So, each day, the battle began to get him to eat.

This was like asking the devil to worship the cross. But, I did not give up finding ways to help my son.

Bruno had a very nice house surrounded by at least four acres of land with a few nice trees. His neighbors were at least 1,000 feet away from his house, providing great privacy. Artur always seemed happy outdoors. But when he would see me bringing out a spoon with his formula, he would say. "No, no, no, no... I am full."

Then, he would clam up. He had to be hungry, though, because he barely ate at all, but he could not stand this formula. Patiently, I tried to give him his first spoonful, but the more I would try, the more he would refuse to take it.

Even though Artur's ability to express himself verbally was limited, it was clear from his actions that he had enormous interest in motorized machines. He had no interest in typical kids' toys, like cars and blocks. He wouldn't touch them. But he was keenly interested in, for example, the window air conditioning unit, which he called **"motor de janela" ("window's motor" in English),** or the swimming pool pump or even the lawn mower. This gave me an idea.

I began to make up stories about these machines, telling him adventures involving him and his family. Hearing these stories, his mouth would gape open in awe and, for the first time, he ate without crying or making faces. Sometimes he even laughed at my anecdotes. As I had to feed him every three hours, I often had to repeat a story that I had already told him. But he didn't like to hear repeated stories or the ones that were not related to

Bruno's machines, so I had to be creative. One day, though, he asked me to repeat the story that I had just told him. At this, he ate twice the normal amount of formula. What a blessing! I could repeat this favorite story over and over again.

> *"Once upon a time, in a very hot place, there was a house that looked like a castle with two people living there, King Bruno and Queen Simone. They had an engine that was placed next to the window."*

When I said this, he always interrupted me and pointed to the air conditioning unit. *"Just like that* **'motor de janela?"**

"Yes. So, the engine was the only source of cold air to cool down the house. This engine could not stop running. If it ever did, people living inside the castle would die. Near their castle, there were some terrible knights who wanted to kill the king and his wife. When they could, these evil knights threw things at the **'motor de janela.'** Whenever this happened, the king called his two royal knights, Sir Artur and Sir Vini. Fast as the wind, they came to King Bruno's aid on their swift horses. King Bruno told them that the evil knights had, once again, tried to destroy the **'motor de janela.'** So, Sir Vini chased and fought the evil knights while Sir Artur got his tools to repair the engine."

At this point, he had eaten at least half of the formula and pushed me to continue. "No! Stop! Dad is going to help Sir Artur, isn't he?"

I took this opportunity to fill his mouth with formula, when the most interesting part of the story was about to come. "Sir Artur then called Sir Papa and together they picked several tools and opened the **'motor de janela.'** When they opened it, the motor was squeaking and making too much noise. Sir Artur and Sir Papa had to get some knives to free the shafts that the evil knights had tried to clog. When they removed everything that was keeping the **'motor de janela'** from running, they realized it was Jasmina's hair…"

He just loved it when I involved Jasmina, his aunt (Soraya's youngest sister), in our adventure and always had a big laugh when I continued.

"Oh, my God, this hair is rotten! We need to move fast. First, we have to save Aunt Jasmina; the bad knights might have kidnapped her. Then, she has to wash her hair; it smells bad, ugh!"

My teacher – King Artur and his daddy - "Sir Idario"

At the end of this story, because of the fictitious bad smell of his aunt's hair, I was making faces and he couldn't stop laughing. When he settled down, he told me that Sir Vini would be enough to save his aunt and that he was responsible for repairing things, not for fighting. It seemed like he was really living this story, and best of all, he ate his formula, not seeming to notice its bad taste or its unappetizing smell.

Artur was finally eating his formula without crying. Sir Papa had triumphed in one more battle.

CHAPTER 30

THE AMAZING DR. STRAUSS

The certainty of having made the right decision

Artur's initial appointment with the liver transplant team at Children's Hospital in Pittsburgh was set. Since the waiting time for a transplant could be lengthy, it was essential that Artur have a qualified MSUD doctor in the States who could monitor his amino acid levels and care for him. So, first, we had to have Artur examined by Dr. Strauss at the Clinic for Special Children. Bruno, our constant ally, would be our driver and translator. With our plans in place, the whole family piled into his car for the three-hour drive to the farmlands near Strasburg, Pennsylvania.

Dr. Strauss greeted us in the reception area at the **Clinic**, and, at seeing Artur for the first time, he paused for a few moments, seeming to be sizing him up on the spot. He then joyfully swept Artur from Soraya's arms and told us just what we wanted to hear.

"You've made the right decision to go ahead with the transplant; I am certain of it. You will see the difference, not only with him but also with your whole family. After the surgery, no more formula, scales, or supplements. They will be in the garbage. Artur will be able to eat real food, just like the rest of the family. MSUD will only be part of your past."

After exchanging a few more words of greeting, Dr. Strauss showed us into one of the exam rooms and began the appointment. He examined Artur thoroughly and took blood samples. Unlike in Brazil where it could take weeks, the results of the blood work came back in a matter of minutes. He reviewed the results and ordered a complete change in Artur's diet, including a new, almost odorless, formula with a pleasant flavor. Looking at Soraya, he continued.

"Don't you worry; I know that you brought lots of the old formula from Brazil. You can donate it to the MSUD Support Group and they will be glad to take it. Until he has the transplant, the Clinic here will provide Artur with this new formula and monitor his care for no charge. Consider this our donation to your cause."

Soraya and I were speechless at this kind gesture. Not being able to express our gratitude in English so well, we could only give him a big hug.

After fighting so many battles in my world, I was in front of the most amazing Samaritan of all!

Artur Santos and the amazing Dr. Strauss - Words from a dictionary are unable to describe these two teachers. One teaches the value of love and the other to compassion.

After the examination, we sat down to meet with Dr. Strauss and discuss everything. Artur and Vinicius were left to roam around the clinic, a place that was custom-made for kids. With his walker, Artur went from room to room, talking to everyone. He didn't care if anyone could understand his weird language; he just wanted to talk. For Vinicius, the toy room was all he needed as he pretended he was in a farmhouse full of wooden toys.

We spent most of the day at the clinic. There, Dr. Strauss explained to us how to feed Artur properly, what kind of medication we should give to him, what kind of natural food he could handle, etc. With Artur's fresh lab results in hand, Dr. Strauss pointed out that his Leucine level was very low, and, to our great surprise, he wanted to give him a half glass of whole milk. We had never tried this before because the Brazilian doctors warned against it, saying Artur could die if he took that much protein. But we were confident in Dr. Strauss and his abilities and knowledge of MSUD, so we agreed. We waited there for a couple of hours to see if he would have a bad reaction, but instead, he asked for more!

At the end of our meeting, Dr. Strauss told us that he wanted to see Artur at least twice a month. He then introduced us to his team and left us to go check on other patients. His team was so professional and friendly; they made us feel so comfortable. In the Clinic's kitchen, Soraya and I got a "hands on" lesson on how to mix the new ingredients for Artur's formula. On his rounds, Dr. Strauss stuck his head into the kitchen to check on us:

"How are you guys doing? Did mom prepare some formula? I want to see Soraya preparing the formula and feeding him right now!"

She had just made a day's supply, so I went down the hall to find my nonstop, walking and talking boy and to have him try it. As Dr. Strauss assured us, the new formula was a hit with Artur; he took the whole bottle without any fuss. I just had to promise him that I would tell the "**motor de janela**" story later.

Thanking Dr. Strauss and his team, I told them:

"For me, it feels like we're in heaven. We have the best doctor and the best MSUD team in the world taking care of our son."

Dr. Strauss countered in such a funny way to explaining the difference of dealing with MSUD and having Artur freed from it.

"I wouldn't say that. You are in great hands; we do have a great team here. But, even as we get to know more about MSUD, we'll never be able to balance Artur's amino acids by regulating his diet like a new liver will. And nothing beats natural food. This formula is synthetic, produced in a laboratory. Our bodies are not designed to eat artificial food. So, I suggest you pray that we part company as soon as possible. I am positive that even if we give him the 'dumbest liver' in the world, he will be way better off than if he had ten Dr. Strausses on his side."

After our long and enjoyable day with this amazing man and his team, we loaded Bruno's car with lots of gadgets and cans of new formula and headed back to Virginia. During the drive, I was quiet, thinking.

I have decided: I have to learn English! If not, how will we manage in Pittsburgh? Bruno can't help us forever.

CHAPTER 31

THE OLD PARROT CANNOT TALK!

Really?

In Brazil, we have a proverb: "An old parrot cannot learn how to speak." Really?

A knight who had faced so many battles was now sharpening his weapons for a more treacherous battle. To become more independent, I needed to know this terrifying language: English!

I devoted every second of my free time to studying English. But as great as it was to be living at Bruno's house, it wasn't conducive to improving my English. Naturally, everyone there spoke only in Portuguese. Living in the countryside didn't help either; we had almost no contact with Americans. So, I got a dictionary and pulled out some books that Soraya had brought from Brazil and I designed my own English course. I started with irregular verbs. I wrote the present, past and past participles hundreds of times to memorize them.

I also had some English CDs, so I would listen to them when I could. At the beginning, I didn't understand anything. So, I decided to translate them into Portuguese and listen to them every day for a couple of hours. Within a few days, I could understand some of them without having to look at the translations. I would occasionally ask Simone for help, too. She had been in the United States for years and spoke English very well. The more I studied, the more interested I became in learning this weird language.

Some English teachers probably would question my self-teaching methods, but for me, they suited my plan. Writing in English the whole day was like therapy for me. I knew I had to understand this new and difficult language if we were to survive here. Not only that, I had heard that Pittsburgh is a city of few immigrants and I didn't know if we would meet any Brazilians there who could help us.

Gradually, I created English dialogues for everyday situations, like taking a bus, asking for an address, ordering food, etc. I practiced these virtual dialogues and they gave me confidence. But, the most difficult part was to understand the native people in these actual situations. When I had a chance to go out and practice my English, I had in mind how the dialogue should go for a specific situation; however, responses were rarely like the ones I practiced, so I would invariably become tongue-tied and very embarrassed.

My first solo English test was in Pittsburgh on our first visit there. I was relieved that there was a convenience store and some fast food restaurants near our hotel since I had been practicing how to deal with these situations in English. For me, it was cool; I was the one in charge of buying the food and I assumed that I wouldn't have to say much to get what I wanted at these places. In a fast food restaurant, for example, I would look at the pictures, point at or say the number(s) of what I wanted, and I would get my food; very simple. Really? I would pay and everything would be fine. I had even studied how to check that I got the correct change. The plan was perfect...on paper.

In practice, things were quite different. To begin with, people from Pittsburgh talk a little differently from the people in Manassas, VA. My embarrassment was not over.

At McDonald's on my first attempt to buy some food, I nervously walked up to the counter to order, pointing toward the menu displayed behind the counter, and confidently said.

"Number two, please."

"For here or to go? Do you want it as a meal? What size? Do you want sauce?"

When the counter clerk started talking, I got confused right away and I didn't understand a single word. So, with waning confidence I answered back:

"Number two."

She repeated the questions two or three more times until she figured out that I didn't know what she was saying, but that I just wanted food. I did get my food, but really wasn't sure what I was getting. I paid her and accepted the change without even checking it. With my bag of food, I returned to the security of my hotel room to practice my food-ordering technique again.

By the third day in Pittsburgh, we were tired of eating sandwiches. I practiced and then went out to order some salad. I thought it would be easy. The name in English is pretty much the same as in Portuguese, "salada." However, when I ordered it, the clerk asked me:

"What kind of **dressing?**"

I just kept saying "Caesar salad." She couldn't even understand my "Caesar" pronunciation and I thought that she was offering me some clothes, dresses I figured, but why would I want that? So, I just replied.

"No dresses! No dresses!"

So, my order came without "dresses" and I ate the most tasteless salad ever. In Brazil, aside from the Portuguese word for "dressing," "molho," being very different from English, if you order a salad, most restaurants have a designated dressing for each salad and you rarely have to order it specifically.

I can't say that I learned English in a month, but the time spent at Bruno's house gave me a good start.

On, on our second visit to Pittsburgh, I met a wonderful volunteer from the Greater Pittsburgh Literacy Council, who helped me tremendously.

After several more months of study and practical use, the "**old parrot**" was able to communicate in English.

Oh, YEAH!

CHAPTER 32

THE PROMISED LAND

Here we go, Steelers

In mid-July 2005, we arrived in Pittsburgh to await for the transplant. Pittsburgh is a beautiful city in southwestern Pennsylvania. Learning about Pittsburgh had been one of my English lessons, so I was somewhat familiar with the city. Pittsburgh is known as a steel city because it was the historical hub of the US iron and steel industry. Pittsburgh is now known for its world-class medical facilities. The world's first liver transplantation was successfully performed there, as well as the first simultaneous heart, liver, and kidney transplant. Also, The Robotics Institute at Carnegie Mellon University, established to conduct basic and applied research in robotic technology for industrial and societal applications, was the first of its kind in the world.

The Big Mac, which is the signature sandwich at McDonald's fast food restaurant chain, was "invented" by Pittsburgh-area restaurant owner, Jim Delligatti, and was test marketed in three Pittsburgh-area McDonald's restaurants in 1967. By 1968, it had become a mainstay on McDonald's menus throughout the country. Dr. David Strickler, a pharmacist, made the first banana split in Pittsburgh.

Pittsburgh holds honors in American sports history, hosting the first baseball World Series game in 1903. On November 2, 1920, Pittsburgh radio station KDKA became the first commercial radio to hit the airwaves and it is still broadcasting.

Pittsburgh's unique landscape amazed me. The city grew among rivers, hills, and valleys. Finding flat land anywhere is not an easy task. With 446 bridges, Pittsburgh is also known as the "city of bridges," having the most bridges of any city in the world, even beating out Venice, Italy. The unique design of many of these steel bridges enhances the already fascinating city view. Inbound from the airport, it was unforgettable when exiting the darkness of the Fort Pitt Tunnel, one of several major tunnels in the city, to be welcomed by a breath-taking view of the downtown and its three rivers.

These are just a few of the reasons why Pittsburgh holds an important status in the United States. Even more significant to me, Pittsburgh changed my mind about the American people. I came to the United States with the idea that all Americans were cold, arrogant people. This is what most Brazilians thought, so did I. But even though I couldn't speak their language very well, most people seemed to be friendly. My first impression was very positive about this amazing city.

We stayed at the Wyndham Hotel in a neighborhood called Oakland, which is in the heart of the city's academic and medical complex. Children's Hospital was just a block away from our hotel and downtown was just a short bus ride away. The streets in Oakland were surprisingly busy even though it was summer. We saw quite a few students, doctors and other medical workers in their white smocks or scrubs and others wearing black and yellow shirts and/or jerseys with a big letter P on it. It seemed to me that Oakland was a lively neighborhood.

I soon came to know why the black and yellow colors were so dominant in weird hats, extravagant clothes, and even some cars! I had heard of American football, but didn't know anything about it except that it just seemed to be a brutal game. However, when I came to know this sport, I immediately became addicted to it and immediately became part of the **Steelers Nation.** The Steelers are Pittsburgh's professional football team.

After three days becoming familiar with the wonderful city of Pittsburgh (eating sandwiches and salads with no "dresses"), it was time to take care of business: Artur's evaluation day arrived.

Without Bruno's help, I was really worried about my English and how I would deal with the transplant team.

Since Children's Hospital of Pittsburgh (CHP) is a huge facility, I thought we would have some problems getting oriented there. So, Bruno had written a note for us to ask to be guided to the transplant department. We stopped first at the emergency entrance and showed the note to the nurse there who called a police officer. Every move generated fear and distrust. However, the officer was there to escort us to the seventh floor.

There, we waited briefly for the doctor. Dr. George Mazariegos, is the director of pediatric transplantation at CHP and, by the grace of God, he speaks Spanish. So, I immediately felt comfortable. He, of course, was aware of Artur's basic medical history, but Dr. Strauss had also filled him in about our long and frustrating journey. He was also aware that we didn't speak English very well, so, he arranged for a translator for the entire evaluation.

What a different world!

My first impression of Dr. Mazariegos was that he was a very calm, good-hearted man, just as Dr. Strauss had told us. Compared to our experience with some Brazilian doctors, Dr. Mazariegos was immediately a breath of fresh air. We had suffered so much with some Brazilian doctors; we didn't need to face that again, especially since we didn't know the language here.

As it turns out, our translator, Ines, spoke Spanish, which wasn't a problem for me. But Soraya couldn't understand anything. So, I became Soraya's translator. It was like a game of "tag" with languages.

Artur's evaluation began with a test of his cognitive skills. The transplant team explained that they would not do a transplant to cure MSUD if the brain had been severely damaged, in which case the MSUD kid could not develop intellectually. But after hours of testing, the doctor said that Artur was very intelligent, but his development had some delays, especially in his speech, a condition that responds well through therapy. His motor skills were tested next. Even though he was three years old, he used a walker to ambulate. Back in Brazil, when he was two years old, he had been taking some steps on his own; however, an MSUD crisis caused by an imbalance in his amino acid levels resulted in losing a lot of this ability. The doctor was confident, though, that Artur could progress on his walking with intensive therapy.

As the week passed, our little king had numerous other tests. He hated giving blood samples; the stinging caused him so much discomfort.

Reviewing his current drug regimen, the doctors dropped a seizure drug called Phenobarbital because of potential side effects on his new liver and replaced it with one called Kapra with fewer possible problems.

Ines helped us to get a room in The Family House, a hotel-like place that is like a "home away from home" for families in town for medical purposes. Even more important, it was far cheaper than our hotel room and on the same street! At The Family House, we would be living with families with members who were recovering from inpatient treatment or waiting for a transplant. There, we met interesting American people and people from all over the world. In the communal kitchen there, we would share food and our experiences.

For one of our appointments, Ines, our interpreter didn't show up. One of the coordinators knew a medical research physician who was working at a nearby hospital and called her to fill in. In the transplant department lobby, a pretty woman came and introduced herself as Dr. Camila Macedo. She told us, in Portuguese, that she was from São Paulo and she would be our interpreter for today! Soraya was ecstatic! Finally, she could understand the translations first-hand. Camila was so sweet, and, almost immediately, became a close friend and confidant. She became so special to us that later she accepted our invitation to be Artur's godmother.

At the end of an exhaustive week and worried that CHP could request more money from me, I requested a meeting with CHP's financial department. Dr. Camila translated for me. At the end of our meeting, my major concern was gone. Mr. Hartman told me that the Stamps Foundation, a non-profit organization that helps kids with MSUD, had allocated money for two kids, including Artur, and I should not be concerned. It was all covered, even possible unanticipated events.

After all of the medical tests and evaluations were done, we had a meeting with the pediatric transplant coordinators to discuss the risks of the surgery and the procedure during the time we would be waiting for a donor.

During the waiting period, we had to have an open communication line with the team 24/7. So, we got a cell phone. In case we planned to be outside of Pittsburgh during this waiting period, the team needed to know the addresses and phone numbers of our possible destinations, all of this to be sure that we could be reached at any time. If we got a call that a liver was available, we had to get to the hospital within eight hours from their call; otherwise, the organ would be donated to another patient. We should also be prepared for "false" calls. In other words, they could call us and schedule the surgery, but cancel the procedure for various reasons, including the donor organ's condition, Artur's health at that time, the organ size, etc.

After about two weeks, Artur was now officially on the United States organ waiting list.

It was too much information at once. Even though I was very concerned about this major surgery, I was still convinced that we were doing the right thing. When we first visited Dr. Strauss back in 2004, only four MSUD patients had been transplanted. Little more than one year later, CHP had done about 14 of these transplants. I had a chance to talk to a teenager who had undergone a transplant recently; he was very happy.

"I am very confident about my future. To be cured from MSUD was not my parents' call; I decided to go ahead with it. Of course, they had to give permission for it. I am glad that everything went well. It has been little more than a month, and now I am eating everything. I already feel the difference. I can concentrate much better, and, socially, my friends accept me better. I don't have to sit at the table with them and look at them eating sandwiches while I could only eat formula from a bottle that I had to carry everywhere with me."

Not only that, he only had to take a small pill to prevent rejection. Showing me the pill, he continued.

"This is a very small capsule. Can you see it? It is at least 10,000 times smaller than my old MSUD bottle. I take this pill with a sip of water and I am good for the rest of the day."

Talking to this kid was such a blessing. His positive attitude only reinforced our commitment to save our little king.

CHAPTER 33

THE WAIT

Every time the phone rang, my heartbeat skyrocketed.

When the evaluation was concluded and my son was on the transplant list, we went to wait at our friend's house in Virginia. There, some disturbing thoughts were tumbling through my mind, mainly that my son's life depended on somebody else's death, a child's no less. This was hard to come to grips with. Just when suffering the pain of losing a child, a donor's parents would have to decide whether to donate their child's organs to a stranger.

Would it even happen?

So many thoughts like these ran through my mind during these otherwise leisurely days. That, combined with the intensity of just waiting around, made me unable to sleep well. Even though we were comfortably living in Bruno and Simone's home in Virginia, waiting for the transplant was not an easy task.

When the phone rang at Simone's house, everyone would tense up. After a week of waiting, the hospital called to say that Artur was moving fast toward the top of the United States waiting list. We understood that in the United States, MSUD is considered a high-risk disease, so moving up on the list was not unexpected. Even so, this call made us more nervous.

One thing that kept us occupied was Artur's condition. He had to remain healthy during this waiting period by eating well, avoiding accidents, like falling or hurting himself, and, most importantly, not getting any cold or infection. His condition had to be good when the call came or else he would be ineligible for his transplant.

We had an appointment scheduled with Dr. Strauss on August 26, 2005. Simone was our driver this time. At the Clinic, Dr. Strauss asked Soraya,

"Are you ready to go to Pittsburgh? They just called me."

"Yes, we are. But, you're kidding me, aren't you?"

Laughing, he continued.

"Yes, I just wanted to see your reaction. It will happen just like that, though. You never know when they'll call. So, are you ready?"

"Yes, we've been well-trained by the transplant team. Our bags are packed and we're ready to move on a moment's notice."

"Great, I am glad to hear that. Now, let's look at this boy."

He was amazed with Artur's development.

"Have you noticed how different Artur is today compared to when you first brought him here? I can tell you, it will be only a matter of weeks and he will be walking without help. He is healthy and growing. Let's keep him on his current diet. It's working great for him, don't you think?"

"Definitely, yes, thanks entirely to you!"

"You don't have to thank me. You've come all the way from Brazil, so I think you deserve the best team in the world to take care of your son. Being part of your story is a blessing for me. I am the one who should thank you."

The more we got to know Dr. Strauss, the more extraordinary he became to us. He became the Santos family savior.

Our roundtrip to Strasburg to see Dr. Strauss was more than 300 miles, so everybody was exhausted by the time we got back to Simone's house. We ate a late dinner and went straight to bed. Then at about 7:15 am:

"Riiiiing, Riiiiing..."

It was the house phone. I'd heard something and thought I was dreaming. But when Simone knocked on our door, I immediately knew that something was up.

"It's Children's Hospital. They are asking if you are ready."

Soraya leaped out of bed, excited.

"What?"

"The transplant team is on the line. They have an organ for Artur!"

"Tell them we're on our way!" shouted Soraya.

Even though we had our transport plan in place, it was chaos nevertheless. Having plans on paper was very simple and they seemed easy to execute, but we didn't plan for the emotional aspects of getting "the call." And to top it off, it was raining cats and dogs! So, we took a deep breath and tried to be calm, but still, tears were flowing again.

Our packed bags were still in Simone's car. Soraya went to prepare some formula. Simone woke up Bruno and then, we had a little meeting. Within our plan "A", Bruno would be our driver from his house to Pittsburgh. Instead, he said that he was not emotionally able to drive us to Pittsburgh. He continued:

"Besides, we have a severe storm and I am afraid of getting stuck in traffic and not making it to the hospital on time."

So, we reserved a flight from Washington, DC to Pittsburgh at 11:15 am that morning.

Children's Hospital kept in frequent contact with us that day. We woke up Artur and got him ready to go. But what to do with Vinicius? Unbelievably, we hadn't thought about what we should do with him…take him with us or leave him with Simone? Simone quickly suggested. "If he goes with you, he could not help and hospitals usually do not allow kids in ICUs. You better leave him here. I'll take care of him."

At 9:45 am, we headed to the airport with Bruno at the wheel of his VW Passat moving as fast as he could.

Artur seemed blissfully happy; he knew that we were going to the airport and he loved flying on these "metal birds." So, he was the calmest of all of us.

When we arrived at the airport, Bruno helped with our check-in and hung around with us until we were on board. He wanted to be sure that we were on that plane before he went to work.

Wouldn't you know it! A severe storm in the area was delaying our flight by several hours. We were frantic...we might miss this transplant opportunity. We called the hospital and told them about the delay. They asked us to wait and they would get back to us. Just about half an hour later, we heard Artur's name in an airport announcement. Bruno didn't quite understand what they said. So we went to the information desk. Children's Hospital had arranged another flight for us and we needed to move quickly.

It was almost 1:00 pm when we finally got into the airplane heading to Pittsburgh. On our way, we could finally gather our thoughts. Soraya was able to contain her emotions and then she began talking to Artur, comparing his liver to a toy battery. She told him,

"Artur, your inside 'battery' is not working properly. So, when we get to Pittsburgh, the doctor will put you to sleep and he will replace your battery. You will stay for a little while in the hospital and then, you will be able to eat everything, just like your brother."

"Is the doctor going to sting me?"

"Probably, but, it will be fast and he will need to do it to replace your battery. You won't feel anything. Just relax and remember that mom and dad will be always with you."

"Can I hold your hand?"

"Yes, your dad and I will be holding your hand all the time. Isn't that right, dad?"

"Yes. Mom is right; we will be with you all day long."

Soraya's loving way of explaining everything to Artur was very interesting and made me feel relieved. But, behind their backs, I could not stop crying.

When we arrived at the Pittsburgh airport, the rain was heavier than in Washington, but, luckily, Children's Hospital had advised the ground crew, and they gave us priority to disembark. I could speak a little English at this point, which helped to explain to the taxi driver that we needed to get to Children's Hospital as quickly as possible.

We thought we had a good plan for the day we got "the call." But you can't plan the weather, so this day had almost turned into a nightmare.

Thank God, it didn't!

CHAPTER 34
THE CRUCIAL MOMENT

A cure: finally we heard the word we'd been waiting for.

Check-in at Children's Hospital was stressful in itself, but my anxiety only increased as I began to realize just what was about to happen. So much so that I prayed that this would turn into a false call, that the donor liver would not be suitable for Artur for some reason. I've never felt such fear in my life. But, I tried to stay calm for Soraya and Artur's sakes.

On the transplant floor, nurses were preparing Artur for surgery while trying to explain the procedures to us. But, I was so nervous that I just couldn't think in English. So, one of the nurses called a Brazilian whom she knew was in the hospital with his daughter.

A few minutes later, João Galvão, a Brazilian-American, arrived to help us. Speaking perfect English to the nurses and translating for us in perfect Portuguese, we became calmer as he managed to clearly explain the procedures. João Galvão was an amazing help to us.

The clock struck six o'clock in the evening on August 27, 2005. Our **king** was taken into the operating room to overcome this terrible disease. I asked God to protect Artur and make sure that this was not the last time that I would see him. With great trepidation and tears of hope, we left him in the hands of the doctors. A transplant coordinator showed us to a waiting room and reassured us.

"Everything will be fine; just be prepared for a long surgery. That's normal and a doctor will try to come out and update you on their progress."

Hours later, we overheard somebody asking for the Santos family. It was Dr. Mazariegos, the head of the Children's Hospital transplant unit whom we had met during the evaluation. Speaking in Spanish, he told us,

"Artur's new liver is in place and is already working on its own. Everything is going well. My team is now tying in the blood vessels; this is a tedious part of the surgery because there are so many and they are very tiny. After that, we'll close his abdomen. So, we have several more hours to go, but I just wanted you to know that Artur is cured. His new liver guarantees that."

I just wanted to see and to touch my son. But Dr. Mazariegos said the words that we had been waiting so long to hear … **Artur is cured.**

At that moment, I was thrilled, I had found the maze's exit, and at the end of it, I was going to claim my Grail. But in a few moments, another wall of uncertainty was about to block our exit. I had seen the Grail, but it seemed that I needed a little more time to grasp it in my hands.

An hour later, we heard some shouting in the outer area of the waiting room. It grabbed our attention because it was loud and it was in Portuguese.

"I am looking for Guarana, Brazil, Botucatu…"

To hear this in Portuguese was quite funny for us. Those words were not forming a single phrase, and so, they were making no sense at all. So, I stood and investigated. It was a young guy, a doctor for sure because he was wearing scrubs. He had a big smile on his face. When I got closer to him, I realized it was Dr. Kyle Soltys. I had seen his picture in the transplant team brochure during the evaluation and his young face was easy to recognize. Dr. Soltys apparently knew about our issues with English. So, he continued, speaking slowly in English this time. He introduced himself and apologized.

"Hi. I am Dr. Kyle Soltys. I'm sorry, I wish I could speak more Portuguese, but these are the only words I know. I know they don't make sense together, but I like to say them anyway. Now, let's talk about your son. We are still working on tying in his blood vessels. And it's going well. His new liver is working well; it's just a bit larger than his old one, a little too large to fit easily into his belly area."

Gesturing with his hands and pointing to his own belly, Dr. Kyle continued his explanation. "Because of the size of the new liver, we will not suture his belly muscles back together right now. We will only close the outer skin, and his belly muscles will remain open until he grows enough to hold the new liver comfortably. This is not unusual in a surgery like this.

I didn't catch everything he said, but I understood enough to be scared. I tried to translate for Soraya, and we both thought it was very strange. Our exit from the maze was being blocked again. But we had great confidence in this transplant team, so we took it in stride.

At 6:30 am, almost 12 hours of surgery later, Artur was finally taken to the recovery room. The surgery was done and he would soon be transferred to the ICU. It was not a pretty sight. He was very swollen all over. The nurse lifted the sheet so we could see his stitches. His stomach was huge. It looked like he was at least eight pounds over his normal weight. He had so many medical and monitoring devices attached that it was difficult to even touch him. I counted more than sixteen pumps injecting drugs into his body. At the ICU, we were introduced to Dr. Bond, another physician from the transplant team and the one in charge here.

Camila arrived in the ICU soon after us. As we were talking, I saw blood coming out of one of Artur's draining tubes and pointed it out to Camila. Her reaction was immediate. She ran for Dr. Bond, and he quickly started a plasma transfusion. The scene was a bit chaotic, but Camila still was able to explain that Artur was bleeding internally and that he may have to return to the operating room if it can't be stopped. Meanwhile, Dr. Bond was working hard to control this bleeding. Fortunately, the bleeding did stop in a few minutes and Artur didn't have to go back into surgery.

CHAPTER 35

WHY HIM?

Now, the Grail seemed far in the distance

On the third day after his transplant, Artur's situation was only getting worse. He fell into a coma, again. Doctors were at his side constantly, specialists of every type. The kidney specialist told me that the transplant had apparently altered his renal function and that they were dealing with it. Even with the language barrier, it was clear that Artur's life was again in danger.

Several days went by with no good news. Artur was puffy and still not moving at all. When the nurses put him on his side to bathe him, a large bed sore on his back was getting worse and he was losing his hair.

Why? Why is this happening to my king?

It had been over a week since we had arrived in Pittsburgh. We had been in contact with Simone and knew that Vinicius was missing us. He needed to be here in Pittsburgh, but we couldn't easily take off for Virginia. Realizing our predicament, Dr. Camila, always on our side, dropped everything and drove to Virginia herself to pick Vinicius up and bring him to us. Camila never ceased to amaze us. With Vinicius in Pittsburgh, our schedule had to be altered a bit. Soraya stayed with Artur during the afternoons, while I took care of Vinicius. Then, at night, we would switch duties, giving each of us a necessary break from the hospital. Just like when we were in Brazil, here in the United States, Soraya or I was with Artur 24/7, a promise that we made to each other some time ago.

My nights in the hospital were quiet. I always liked to go to sleep late. The ICU had a comfortable chair and a TV with many sports channels. Camila was our only regular visitor, and, once in a while, João Galvão would stop by. About this time, the ICU admitted Mihir, the Indian kid with MSUD that we had met at the symposium in Atlanta in 2004. His parents, Nirmal and Mital, were always very nice to us.

After 15 days in the ICU, the doctors decided that Artur should move from the ICU to the semi-intensive care unit. They didn't tell me why they were transferring him. For me, he seemed the same since his surgery, so perhaps it was because of the cost of keeping a patient in the ICU. On the day of the move to the semi-ICU, the doctor on duty noticed that Artur was breathing with difficulty. He asked me who authorized Artur's move, but I had no answer for this new doctor.

This day, the doctor in the semi-ICU, saved Artur's life. He noticed that I understood little English, so very slowly, he told me that he thought something could be compressing Artur's lungs. The x-rays and an ultrasound he ordered proved his theory.

Why? Didn't he already have enough?

At this, Artur returned to the ICU. The transplant team, two renal specialists, and several neurologists came daily to monitor his condition. The neurologists' visits, in particular, were even more frequent. Sometimes three or four came at once. Artur was still in a coma and they couldn't figure out what was going on. Even though he was cured of MSUD, his life was now being threatened by an unknown cause. The child from India, who had also had a transplant, was having a remarkable recovery and was already being discharged. I was so happy for him and his family.

But why couldn't Artur be so fortunate?

After a month in the ICU, Artur was still lethargic. At least, most of the machines and some infusion pumps had been removed. From the transplant team's perspective, he had progressed enough to be transferred to the semi-intensive care unit again. After a couple of days in the semi-intensive ICU, Artur was transferred to the seventh floor, which was reserved exclusively for transplanted patients.

We were optimistic when he opened his right eye. But soon after, he began to act strangely. Every night at around 1:00 am, he woke up with a shrill cry. The cry was so intense that, when it happened for the first time, it scared me to death. I could see in the monitor that his heart rate had rapidly increased. A nurse gave him some pain medicine, but still he cried for hours. I would then pat his butt to try to calm him down until he returned to the lethargic state that had become his normal condition.

Nights like these became routine and they terrified me. Like clockwork, each episode would start just after midnight, so I prepared for them by standing by his side at that time. After several of these episodes, I suggested to the nurse to give him some morphine, but the nurse refused my request. Camila intervened and the transplant team allowed him to have some morphine. But the situation only got worse. He seemed to be in severe pain.

His pain was so intense. Ours was immeasurable.

CHAPTER 36

THE AMAZING DR. STRAUSS STRIKES BACK

Only a Superman could save my son.

At this point, I had lost track of time. Artur had been in this coma for almost two months with no breakthroughs. My desperation was only increasing. Fortunately, we had Camila for support. And despite everything, I was still confident that God would not abandon us. And He has expressed himself in many ways, even thru friends' advice.

Unexpectedly, Mihir, the Indian kid who got a new liver a week after Artur, was admitted back to the seventh floor. When his father Nirmal came to visit me, we talked a little about our sons when all of sudden, he asked:

"Why don't you call Dr. Strauss? Maybe he can help you."

It was a Sunday morning when Nirmal gave me this advice. But I was apprehensive and wondered what I would say to Dr. Strauss. After all, he deals with kids who have MSUD, not with kids, like Artur, who have had the transplant and been cured. And how I would communicate with him? My English was still poor. So, I decided that I wouldn't bother him.

That night, my friend, João Galvão, came to visit us. Minutes later, Nirmal entered into our room and told us that the doctors were pleased with his son's progress and that they would be leaving the hospital soon. As we continued talking, about Artur now, Nirmal encouraged me again to call Dr. Strauss, this time with the full support of João Galvão. Procrastinating even further, I told them,

"I better call him tomorrow. Today is Sunday and its 9:30 pm. He's probably asleep and I don't want to bother him. Besides, I don't have his number here with me and he might not understand my broken English."

Frustrated with me, Nirmal practically forced the phone into my hand to call Dr. Strauss right then. He had Dr. Strauss' phone number and João Galvão volunteered to talk to him on my behalf.

I dialed Strauss' number. He answered the phone with a hoarse voice:

"Hello!"

"Dr. Strauss? This is Santos, Artur's father. How are you doing?"

"Who?"

"Santos, from Brazil. Remember?"
"Oh! Yes, what's going on?"

With my broken English I continued:

"I am sorry to bother you. I know it is Sunday and you perhaps were asleep. I am going to pass the phone to my friend. He'll explain better what is going on."

Through me, João Galvão explained to Dr. Strauss that Artur had been in a coma for almost 8 weeks and the transplant team, along with some neurologists, couldn't figure out what was going on with him.

Wide awake by now, Dr. Strauss told us that he would consult with Dr. Mazariegos and get back to me by the following Thursday. He then asked to speak to me.

"You don't have to apologize. Everything will be fine; give me a few days and I'll see what I can do for Artur."

The next morning, I was going down to the cafeteria to buy a cup of coffee when, to my utter shock, I met Dr. Strauss at the elevator. I couldn't believe it was him!

"Dr. Strauss? Is that you? Oh, my God, I can't believe it."

"Yes, it's me. I am glad that I found you. I am kind of lost looking for your son."

"But you told me that you would be calling by Thursday?"

"You're right, but when I hung up the phone last night, I couldn't sleep. I talked with my wife and I explained that you were in trouble. So, I put myself in your place. I knew I couldn't focus on my work back at the clinic without trying to resolve this situation with Artur. I had already talked with Mazariegos and he gave me the "green light" to work on your son's case. So, I jumped in my car and drove to Pittsburgh. I just need you to find someone to translate for us. My Portuguese is very bad."

As he laughed at his own joke, I picked up my phone and called Camila, our Brazilian friend who was at the adjacent Presbyterian Hospital. She immediately came to meet us on the 7th floor. Confidently, Dr. Strauss took control.

"Take me to see Artur."

I guided Dr. Strauss and Camila to Artur. After a brief exchange, he and Camilla went in search of Artur's file. With emotions welling up, I stayed with my son.

When I calmed down, I called Soraya and told her that Dr. Strauss was here to help Artur.

"Come here ASAP; he might need to talk to us."

Soraya arrived at noon, and we waited until Dr. Strauss and Camilla returned to our room. Late that afternoon, after greeting us, he took a sheet of paper and drew three double-arrow lines in the shape of a triangle.

"Artur is in a coma because of these three complicating factors. First, due to his poor kidney function, his body is retaining fluid. Second, Kapra is one of his meds and it is interfering with his brain functions. These two conditions combined to cause a third condition called

Leukoencephalopathy, which is a bubble of fluid in Artur's brain, and this bubble is acting like a tumor. The episodes of screaming at night are definitely associated with severe pain caused by this tumor."

Soraya, very distressed, asked, "What can be done? Does this tumor mean that he could have some brain damage? Please be honest with me."

He picked up his pen and on the same paper he wrote REVERSIBLE. He then continued,

"I've seen this before and I know that this Leukoencephalopathy is reversible. We first need to stop the morphine before he becomes addicted to it. Since I'm not on staff here, I'll have to discuss this with Mazariegos. If he and his team agree with my conclusions and go with my treatment plan, Artur will improve dramatically in a week or so."

Dr. Strauss also told me that if Artur had any brain damage, it would have been caused by MSUD, not by the liver transplant or by this reversible Leukoencephalopathy.

After his kind words, Dr. Strauss said goodbye to everyone, checked in on Artur one more time, and prepared to leave the hospital. I then asked about the cost of his visit. He smiled and said that God already paid for his visit.

"Don't worry. Everything will be fine, and you can call me at any time. I feel responsible for you guys and I am glad that we're honing in on what's going on with him."

I couldn't thank him enough. I was so impressed. Dr. Strauss was only a casual acquaintance and he drove a total of ten hours, devoted his entire day to a foreign kid's case, and everything was done at no charge. His kindness left me speechless. Even though he was in pain and motionless, our **king** seemed to have a very strong aura about him that attracted great people like Dr. Strauss.

Later that evening, he called Camila and told her that the transplant team had agreed with his recommendations. We could now expect things to change right away.

Two days later, Artur was showing signs of improvement, moving his body and even opening his eyes.

Within a week, Artur was still weak, but his body movements continued to improve. After such a positive reaction, his clinical status was considered stable and the terrible night screams had decreased. By now, he was almost 4 years old, and again, he had lost the ability to chew and swallow. Our dreams of seeing him eating normal food had to be delayed and he had to continue being fed through a nasal tube.

Even though he was awake, and his movements had been improving day by day, he was far from being considered a normal child. Right before his transplant, he was almost walking by himself and now, he couldn't even hold his body erect. He couldn't even sit down on his own. With Dr. Strauss' recommendations, the fluid buildup was gone. So, he began to look like a malnourished child. The hospital then recommended that he go through intensive physical therapy. A talented physical therapist at the hospital worked with him every day. But with his nerves and joints in a state of atrophy, he still seemed to be in great pain and hated these sessions.

As Artur's condition improved, the doctors' visits became less frequent and the neurologists and kidney specialists had disappeared. Only the transplant team and the physical therapist were coming every morning to check on our son.

Even though Artur was awake and somewhat less lethargic, he didn't talk at all and he was getting thinner and thinner. So, his transplant team decided to transfer him to a nearby intensive rehabilitation center that was outside the hospital. At first, I was really worried about this move. I felt our son was being abandoned and wondered if money was the real reason for the move and if we would lose contact with the transplant team.

My many concerns about this move were partially relieved after Camila talked to the transplant team.

No need to worry; the hospital is still responsible for your son. They are not abandoning him. Artur's care is their top priority. So get ready because they will be transferring him very soon.

I thought I was prepared for everything; however, I was not emotionally ready to see my son leave the hospital.

Sir Papa could do nothing but cry!

CHAPTER 37

BACK TO THE MAZE

Only God knew what was about to come

Would Artur become one of its many Amazing Kids?

This is what I thought when Artur and I boarded an ambulance heading for the Children's Institute, a medical rehabilitation center for kids in a nearby Pittsburgh neighborhood. I was concerned about the transfer from the familiar, safe environment of the hospital to this unknown place. But, the coordinator at Children's Institute of Pittsburgh (CI), broke the ice.

"Mr. Santos, our place is known for its **Amazing Kids**. That's because you cannot imagine what our team and our kids are capable of. I have personally witnessed some miracles. Plus, Artur will return to Children's Hospital each week for evaluation by the transplant team. We also have doctors on staff here who will communicate with the transplant team as needed."

Phew! Sir Papa and King Artur were prepared for another fight and once again with renewed hope.

One of our many concerns was whether Artur would ever be able to walk without assistance. When we asked, the CI doctor replied,

"It's difficult to determine this at such an early stage. We have seen worse cases here and have had very good results. With intensive therapy and medications, we'll do our best to help your son."

Artur was still on a feeding tube. The speech therapist explained that due to his coma, his facial muscles had also atrophied and he had lost his sucking ability, but they expressed confidence that these movements will come back to normal. The CI team told us that Artur's arms and legs would need to be gently stretched from their contracted position by using special orthopedic equipment, like splints and braces. We agreed with everything, and only then did my fear of the unknown begin to decline. Camila assured us that we were in good hands. With sweet words, she also tried to comfort Soraya.

I was concerned not only about my son. Who is going to pay for this treatment?

Concluding the evaluation, we met Denise De Felice, a CI coordinator, and Christine Meier, the CI social worker. Denise went on to tell us that Artur's expenses would be covered by Children's Hospital and that all medical procedures would be in accordance with the protocol established by Children's Hospital's transplant team. Christine explained that, as our social worker, she would be available to help make us more comfortable in any way she could; all we needed to do was ask.

My fears had evaporated. I felt confident that this move to the Children's Institute was a wise decision. Soraya was calm and Camila was on our side as always. Only God knew what was about to come, but we were beginning to feel more comfortable with the whole situation.

Artur cried inconsolably on his first day of therapies. He was in pain and all I could do was try to comfort him.

"My son, just relax. Don't be afraid, I'll be with you all the time. These people are trying to help you. They have to put these splints on you and you must try to work with them. Mom is with your brother and she will be here later today."

After days of intensive therapy and a lot of crying, the doctor decided to inject Botox into Artur's legs, telling us that it would relax his muscles and help him to extend his legs.

With our consent, the CI doctor injected Botox all over his thighs. Poor Artur, again he was crying uncontrollably. I could not stand seeing so much suffering, and, for Soraya, it was even worse. Since Artur was born, she hadn't had much joy with her beloved son.

Two days after the Botox injections, we could see some great results. Artur was finally stretching his legs. The therapists tried to put him in a standing position, but he was not strong enough to hold up his own body weight. They brought an apparatus called a "stander." It was like a stretcher that could hold a kid either horizontally or vertically. They laid him down on the stander, tied him in with straps, and cranked up the apparatus so that he was in an upright position. Since the transplant, this was the first time that we saw our son in a vertical position. Within a few days, the therapist managed to put him upright on a bare floor and he could support his body holding a walker that we had brought from Brazil. He even tried to take a few steps.

Back and forth, Artur had periods of successes and failures. His arms were moving more easily, and he began to play. After two months of speech therapy, he began to drink fluids.

Artur, however, was still silent and with a vague look on his face.

CHAPTER 38

THE PERFECT PLAN

♫ Blond Parrot with a golden beak
Take this little letter to my girlfriend.
If she's asleep, knock on the door,
If she's awake, leave this message... ♫

I needed to find a way to break Artur's silence. I came up with a plan, but was reluctant to share it with Soraya. I was afraid that she would never agree. I knew it was risky, but it would be a perfect plan. Every week, Artur had an appointment with the transplant team at Children's Hospital. This appointment quickly became a routine event for us. An ambulance would pick us up at Children's Institute and drop us off at the ER entrance of the hospital. We would prearrange a pick up time with the ambulance driver for our return to Children's Institute after the checkup.

On November 28, 2005, the day of one of Artur's weekly appointments at Children's, I delayed our return a bit because of my plan. Sir Vinicius went with us that day, so he was in on the plan. After Artur's appointment, my plan was to have lunch at Wendy's just across the street from the hospital. We had to keep it a secret from Soraya because she would never agree to take Artur where he could be exposed to any sickness. So I decided to spring it on her at the last second.

Before his transplant, Artur loved to go to Wendy's. But the only food that he could eat there was fries. Even so, he loved Wendy's, maybe because it was a change from his formula or for the free kid's meal toys.

My plan came out of the blue a few days before his weekly appointment. I felt that Artur was close to eating some solid food and that he might do better in a different setting. And he certainly could use something to bring some joy to his monotonous life inside this medical bubble. Not only that, but on the day of the transplant, I had promised him that when his "battery" was replaced, I'd take him to Wendy's and he could eat whatever he wanted. He was clearly delighted at that prospect.

Artur's post-surgery complications had kept me from trying to make good on my promise. But even though he was still not eating any solid food and not talking at all, I decided that this would be the day to give it a try. During our appointment, we met our friend, João Galvão, and I invited him to have lunch with us. Soraya still didn't know of my plan. After the appointment, instead of waiting inside for the ambulance, I started walking towards the exit of the hospital when Soraya questioned me.

"Why don't we wait for the ambulance in here like we always do?"

At that point, I had to tell her about my plan. As expected, she didn't agree and was almost shouting,

"Idario, the hospital forbids him to leave; he is still very weak and vulnerable. What if he gets sick? Let's go back inside."

"Don't worry. The hospital doesn't need to know. Besides, it will be a quick lunch and I already asked the ambulance to come later."

Reluctantly, Soraya came along. At Wendy's, I ordered food for everyone, including a good portion of French fries for Artur. At the table with the food, Vinicius took over with his part of the plan. In Portuguese, he started singing Artur's favorite song.

> ♫ *Blond Parrot with a golden beak*
> *Take this little letter to my girlfriend.*
> *If she's asleep, knock on the door,*
> *If she's awake, leave this message...* ♫

As Vinicius performed, Artur almost miraculously seemed to come back to life. His face lit up, and, with a big smile, he sang along with Vinicius:

♪ Blond Parrot with a golden beak

Take this little letter to my girlfriend.

If she's asleep, knock on the door,

If she's awake, leave this message... ♪

Hearing this, tears of joy rolled down our cheeks, even João Galvão's. We couldn't remember the last time Artur had said any words, and here, he was singing! Needless to say, we were causing a lot of commotion. Other customers couldn't understand why two kids were singing in a weird language and the adults were crying. Maybe they thought that the song was sad. My Super Vinicius was the star, following my plan precisely. He had helped his brother with this "magic song," unlocking Artur from his paralyzed state and rekindling our hope for his recovery.

There are people in life that build their personality throughout life and based on influence of others- **Vinicius Santos** *was born with a defined personality. He is an extraordinary son and a real big brother.*

Even though Artur didn't touch his fries, Artur seemed happy.

Two days later, the CI dietary staff sent a meal of grilled chicken and rice for Artur instead of his regular liquid meal. I was kind of surprised, but when he ate everything, I was delighted! The next day, the speech therapist came around with a worried look, asking, "Is Artur hungry? I checked his file and the kitchen sent a solid meal for him yesterday. I didn't order this."

When I showed her the clean plate, she didn't give me a chance to talk. "Did YOU eat the chicken and rice yesterday? What about Artur, what did he eat?"

"No, I had a hot dog and a soda. He ate the whole meal. Wasn't he supposed to?"

"Sure, but I'm just surprised. I thought his mouth movements hadn't improved enough so I hadn't planned on switching him to solid food just yet. And it was an adult portion, wasn't it?"

"Yes, I thought so. But, he didn't stop eating until it was gone. Then, he fell asleep."

For the first time in his life, Artur had eaten a real meal.

CHAPTER 39
GOD'S WATCHFUL EYES

Back home, there are moments of happiness

God was always a certainty for me. After Artur's illness and after so many mazes that I had to pass through, His presence became stronger. My prayers intensified; my certainty that my family was under His eyes grew day by day. With God on our side, we gained strength to face any kind of challenge.

On the same day that Artur was transferred to the Children's Institute, João Galvão introduced me to Joanne Kehris, manager of the Ronald McDonald House of Pittsburgh (RMH). This charitable institution, sponsored by the McDonald's chain of fast food restaurants, has a mission aimed at improving the health and well-being of sick children by offering low-cost bedrooms and/or apartments for these children and their families while they are away from home for medical treatment. This organization provides a home-like setting for families to help them better cope with the often serious medical conditions of their children. And, this was our case.

The RMH was much closer than where we had been living and offered free laundry, telephone, milk, eggs, orange juice, etc., and, at least once a week, local volunteers provided dinner. The RMH facility had two adjacent buildings on the appropriately named Shady Avenue. These structures enhanced the beauty of Pittsburgh's Shadyside neighborhood. One was a red brick colonial style building with 33 hotel-style units along with the administrative offices and two common kitchens, laundry, playroom, etc., and the other building, also a colonial style, had 9 fully furnished and equipped one and two bedroom apartments. Separating the two buildings was a life-size statue of the restaurant's clown mascot, Ronald McDonald, sitting on a bench under a beautiful white dogwood tree. In the backyard, residents could use the grill and the kids could play on the private playground.

We were so pleased that a hotel-style room was available so quickly in the "main" house. This room had two twin beds and a small bathroom, which accommodated us well enough since one of us was always with Artur at the CI. Since we knew that this unit would not work for us, when Artur was discharged, we immediately put our name on the waiting list for an apartment in the next-door building.

The RMH solved our housing problem; however, Vinicius now needed some special help.

As we did with Artur, we did not give up on Vinicius.

The transition to another country was not so easy for our family and, for Vinicius, the turmoil was about to come. When we enrolled him at Springfield Elementary School in Pittsburgh, very often he would come back from school crying, begging us to not send him back to his new school. I went there couple of times to talk to the principal and she always told me that he would be fine.

Besides his language barrier, he told us that he was being bullied by one of his classmates and his teacher would not give him a chance to participate in class.

Vinicius's problems were about to increase when we moved to Ronald McDonald House. To complicate things more, his bus could not pick him up and drop him off at our new address. We went to his school where his principal, who was very friendly, told us, "It is not going be easy for you to find a school with an ESL (English as a Second Language) program like we have. Give me a few days and I'll solve his transportation problem. We want to keep Vinicius here."

Four days later, the principal called and told us that the transportation problem was solved. A cab would pick him up and drop him off at RMH. But, instead of solving the problem, the new ride became a nightmare. Every day, the driver and the cab were different and almost always late. Even worse, they would often forget to bring him back at the end of the school day. On several occasions, I thought Vinicius had been kidnapped.

With all this, Soraya and I decided to take him out of school. Joanne, the Ronald McDonald House Manager, was well aware of our transportation problems and several times she picked up Vinícius in her own car. She was aghast when we told her of our plans to take him out of school.

"You can't do that; he needs to go to school. Let me talk to the Catholic school down the street here and see if they'll accept him at no charge. Just be patient and don't worry. Nobody is going to kidnap your son."

The Catholic school was just two blocks away, but, unlike the public school Vinicius had been attending, the tuition at this school was high. Joanne called Sister Lynn, the principal of Sacred Heart Elementary School, and scheduled a meeting with her. Everything worked better than we could have imagined. Sacred Heart Elementary School became a blessing for Vinícius. As Joanne predicted, after just three months, he was speaking English fluently. We soon began to rely on him to help us understand the language better; he became our in-home English professor. And we could walk him to school and pick him up in less than 3 minutes. He loved this new environment.

Everything in the USA was new for us, even the weather. Pittsburgh weather is totally opposite from our home in Brazil's northeast, where the average temperature is around 90°F and often exceeds 110°F. It is the hottest and driest region of Brazil. We had never seen snow or had faced temperatures below 50°F. So, we were definitely not prepared for this abrupt change. It was October and the temperatures were becoming quite chilly and we were told that the real cold was on its way. Soraya and I wondered how people in Pittsburgh could survive this weather.

December arrived and the weather became unbearably cold for us. We often walked the 1.2 miles from the RMH to the CI, a straight shot, but up and down hills in increasingly colder temperatures. Taking cabs was an option, but cab drivers were not always interested in this short fare. Renting a car would be very expensive and buying one was impossible because our tourist visa status did not allow us to hold a Pennsylvania driver's license and, without that, we couldn't buy a car. The CI was indicating that Artur would be discharged soon and become an outpatient. Would I have to push his wheelchair back and forth from his rehab? Not only that, our room at the RMH was very small and wouldn't hold all four of us, not to mention Artur's wheelchair and other large therapy apparatus. Where would we put this stuff? So, many more problems were on the horizon.

Then, on December 23, we learned that Artur would be discharged from the Children's Institute in just one week, on New Year's Eve. Although I knew this was coming, I still felt some desperation because an apartment still hadn't opened for us at the RHM. I talked to Joanne and, at that point, she couldn't predict when one would be vacated. In preparation for the discharge, I had already told the Children's Institute staff that we could not bring Artur apparatus; there just wasn't enough space in our room at the Ronald McDonald House.

Then, to our great surprise and utter delight, a day before Artur's discharge, Joanne handed me a key for apartment #42, a two-bedroom unit in the adjacent building. God had not forgotten us. The apartment was big enough to fit everybody and Artur's apparatus. We moved in on that same day and the next day, our little **king** was sharing a room with his brother.

Even with our good fortune, we still had to deal with the problem of getting Artur back and forth from his daily outpatient therapy at the CI. For the first time in my life, I saw snow. But, I didn't know if I liked it or hated it. Definitely it is a beautiful season, but it was impossible to push a wheel chair through the snow. Several times, I had to carry Artur on my shoulders and walk the 1.2 miles for his therapy sessions.

It looked like our days of torture would never end. But, once again, God didn't forget us. Nubia, a friend of my sister, Irenice, knowing about our situation, called me saying she had a gift for Artur.

"I have a 1999 Kia Sephia and it's yours if you want it. It's working well and has low mileage. I know how terrible it is to walk in the snow and even worse to be pushing a wheelchair."

I didn't know what to say. "What about you? Don't you need it for yourself?

"No. I'm using my husband's old car and the Kia is just parked here. We're not using it at all. Please take it; all you have to do is come here to pick it up."

"Oh, my God! I can't believe it. You are amazing. How can I thank you?"

"You don't have to thank me. You are a great person and you deserve more than this. I am glad to help."

We had joined St. Hyacinth Catholic Church where we met another angel, Sister Janice, who ran a program that provided support to the Latin community. Not only that, she spoke Portuguese very well as she had been a missionary in the Brazilian Amazon for more than four years. She took care of all the paperwork to temporarily transfer Nubia's car to the church. With my international driver's license, I could drive this amazing gift and, thanks to Nubia and Sister Janice, our commute to Artur's therapy became short and easy.

God did not take His eyes of our family. He strengthened and encouraged us any time new problems arose.

And they arose. The snow was just one of them.

CHAPTER 40

THE AMERICAN IMMIGRATION SYSTEM AND THE NEUMEYERS

A complicated battlefield

Artur's current condition and his ongoing need for medical care were leading us down a different avenue than we had been considering when we arrived in the United States. Our plan was always to return to Brazil. But Dr. Strauss advised me that I really should be preparing to plan to live in the United States for some time, until Artur was fully recovered. I needed a job, one that would allow me to support my family with the flexibility to be around for their needs. So, initially, I thought that something part time would give me this flexibility.

Our budget was very tight, but we still had money from Brazil to survive for several months. Little did I know that dealing with the US immigration system would leave us on the edge of financial disaster.

Since my tourist visa did not allow me to work, I had to get a work permit before I could legally take a job in the U.S. I had heard that getting a work permit was so complicated and time-consuming and that working illegally would be so much easier. But I couldn't do it. Growing up, my dad often told me that a real man should put his head on his pillow and sleep soundly without regrets. My parents did not raise me to do illegal things. So, I would not consider this option at all. Not only that, I could not do anything that somehow put Artur's treatment in jeopardy. So, I began the laborious process of finding a legal job.

Ana Paula Carvalho, a Portuguese professor at the University of Pittsburgh, helped me to spread the word regarding my family's necessities and was able to enlist her students to help. A group of students arranged an interview for me with the office of Pennsylvania's U.S. Senator, Arlen Specter. On this occasion, Pedro Bretz, director of the Hispanic Center in Pittsburgh, was also invited for this interview. The senator's assistant seemed to understand a little about immigration laws, telling me that I had to get a job in my field and either the person or company who hired me would need to become my sponsor. I thought to myself, "This will be impossible. Who will want to be responsible for me? I was a nobody here in the United States. Besides that, I had a son with health problems. Who in the world would be responsible for such a family?" To my great fortune, Pedro Bretz knew a lawyer who offered to assist me for free.

Two weeks later, I went with Pedro Bretz to the law firm of Cohen & Grigsby. There, we met a wonderful man, Attorney Larry Lebowitz, who explained the visa process, confirming in extra details what we were told by Senator Specter's assistant. He pointed out that since I was a young and healthy man, I easily cleared the nest hurdle. Dr. Strauss had insisted that Artur not leave the United States right now; therefore, a humanitarian visa would be a possibility, but this type of visa would not permit me to work. So, Attorney Leibowitz thought I should focus on getting a job offer in my field and then apply for the work visa. This would be a better long-term solution for my family.

I thanked him very much, but I confess that I left his office very frustrated. I expected that a visa status existed for those in the U.S. under critical medical care that would also allow me to work. But that was not the case. Nonetheless, the attorney was very kind with positive words and he encouraged me not to give up. Even though I was in "dire straits," I felt Attorney Lebowitz was a source of inspiration. Ana Paula spoke again with her students and they managed to get the University of Pittsburgh to publish an article about Artur. The Institute's staff, along with Pedro Bretz also got an article published by the local newspaper, the Pittsburgh Tribune-Review. Meanwhile, I was searching on the Internet for a job.

After months of searching, I finally got an interview with a botanical garden near Carnegie Mellon University. I was interviewed twice, and when I took the job description to my attorney, he said I would not be qualified for that job. Furthermore, the salary for this position was too low to support my family.

I continued struggling to find a job. Even following our strict budget, money was running short. Our great friends, Angela and Ray, mobilized the Brazilian community in Pittsburgh and many people brought us food, money, and clothes. Sometimes I felt bad about accepting this charity. I was depressed, fearing about our uncertain future. I felt boxed in. I couldn't find a job here and I couldn't leave my family in the U.S. and return to Brazil to start a business or find a job there.

After seven months, I had had a couple of interviews, but they either amounted to nothing or were not in my field. Then, Joanne from the Ronald McDonald House arranged an interview for me with a landscaping company. By this time, I was more confident with my English, and for the first time, I was going to a job interview by myself.

I had a very interesting interview with Mr. Coleman Griffin, owner of the landscaping company. His company was responsible for the design, maintenance, and installation of landscape projects. My job would be to manage some of his employees. While visiting some of his landscaping clients and walking through his facilities, we discussed the possibility of changing my visa status. He agreed to sponsor me and we set up an interview with my attorney. After our interview with my amazing attorney, Larry Lebowitz, we filled out some forms for submission to the US immigration authority. Later that week, I went back to Larry's office to sign some revised documents when my attorney's assistant told me about the visa lottery. I asked, "What lottery?"

"You didn't know? US Immigration Services grants H-1B visas based on a lottery where some 120,000 people apply for a maximum of 65,000 visas available per year. Visas for those applicants who 'win' this lottery will be expedited. I am sorry, didn't you know about this?"

This news was like a bucket of cold water on my expectation of starting work soon. I had never won a lottery and I felt certain that I would not be lucky on this one either. Regardless, I went ahead and submitted my application.

Several months later I got the bad news that I was not selected in the lottery. So, that meant that I would have to wait another year to apply for the H-1B. Mr. Griffin was sympathetic when I told him what had happened and indicated that, if I wanted, we could apply again for next year.

I spent a frustrating year. I even tried going back to school, but how could I support my family while in school? And besides, as my attorney told me, I would still have to go through the same work visa process after finishing my studies.

In 2007, I met with Mr. Griffin and he agreed again to sponsor me for my work visa application. We prepared all the documents and submitted them to the Immigration Service. And to my total surprise, this time I was selected by the lottery. But, in the end I was not approved because, as per the Immigration System, I was overqualified for the position being offered by Mr. Griffin. I knew Soraya was awaiting a response from immigration with the same anxiety as I was. So, after a few days of reflection, I told her that we had to wait another year and that we'd have to save every penny we could since we had only our savings and the generosity of family and friends to live on. And to make matters worse, Artur developed a virus that caused an episode of liver rejection. We had to go back to Children's Hospital where we spent more than a month with him in critical condition.

With this financial nightmare lurking over my head, I had to find another company that could offer me a job that would qualify me for a work visa. I had many chances to work, but the complications of the visa process made possible employers reluctant to sponsor me. In the end, they just gave up on me or told me that their company wasn't equipped to deal with immigration issues of potential employees or they just never called me back.

When Artur was released from the hospital after the viral infection, I talked to Lana Neumeyer, a good-hearted Brazilian who, like us, came to Pittsburgh for medical reasons. Unfortunately, her first husband had passed away due to complications after his surgery. I had heard that she and her new husband owned an environmental company, so I read about it and determined that the soil and water sampling sector could fit me very well. Lana was very friendly and said she would do anything to help me; however, it wouldn't depend solely on her because I had to prove my skills to her husband, Fred Neumeyer, the technical expert in the company. I already knew Fred because he had come to the hospital a couple of times with Lana to visit Artur and Artur loved him. Lana invited me for dinner at their house where Fred told me all about his company and I told him about myself. Fred is a good-hearted man with great wisdom, and by the end of dinner, he agreed to give me a chance.

Together, Lana and I worked hard to prepare the necessary documentation to apply for the work visa. With everything ready, attorney Lebowitz filed my application. However, I was, again, not selected by the lottery. I was in despair. To make things worse, the Ronald McDonald House was about to move to a new location, and understandably, my family could not be accommodated in the new house. So, we quickly had to find another place to live. I knew I could not leave Pittsburgh because of Artur. Our funds were getting shorter and shorter and I had to find a way to support my family. The pressure on me was unbearable. I even considered extreme measures like going into the streets and begging for work or money. Instead, I went into a deep depression. I couldn't get out of bed. After a few weeks, thanks to Soraya, I came back to the real world. I had heard that the immigration rules in Canada were more favorable than the U.S., so I agreed with her to look for a job there. Soraya's sister, Sylvana, hired a lawyer in Toronto and I began searching for a job. It seemed that jobs in my area were easier to find in regions where French was spoken. So, I bought some CDs and started to study French. At the same time, I started the Canadian immigration process.

Even after losing out on the U.S. visa lottery, I didn't lose contact with the Neumeyers or attorney Lebowitz. Both encouraged me to try again. Almost a year had passed and I had not succeeded with my Canadian immigration attempt. It was taking too long and the jobs that I had applied for required personal interviews, but I didn't have a visa to go to Canada. Furthermore, Attorney Lebowitz advised me that even though I was living legally in the U.S., my chances of returning here would probably be lost if I crossed the Canadian border.

My money was quickly evaporating when my father came to the USA to visit my family and, fortunately, he gave me some money. He didn't realize it, but his support was crucial for my family's ongoing necessities.

In April 2009, with the Neumeyers' help, I applied again for an H-1B visa. I told Soraya that this would be our last "shot." I could not stand to go through this again. I was emotionally and financially drained. But, as always, God provided help at the right time. On a Sunday night in August 2009, I looked at the US Immigration website and, to my surprise, I read that my visa had been approved! However, Soraya's and Artur's had been denied. Vini was the only one who didn't need to change his status since he was studying in a private school and had been granted an F1 student visa. I woke up Soraya to give the good and bad news. I told her not to worry because her case could be appealed.

The next day, I called Lana and told her the good news. She was very happy. I then went to Larry's office and asked him to appeal the denial of Soraya and Artur's visa. He filed a new petition and a short time later, their H-4 visas were also granted. Whew, what a complicated battlefield!

Finally, in October 2009, I changed my tourist visa to an H-1B work visa. Today, we all have Green Cards granting us Permanent Resident Status and I continue working for Neumeyer Environmental Services, Inc. Larry Lebowitz, besides being a great attorney and a great person, he is a great friend whom we will never forget. The same goes for the Neumeyers who are now part of my family. Without these amazing people, I do not know what would have happened to my family.

CHAPTER 41

THE FIRST STEP TOWARD A NEW LIFE

I had to believe in my instincts

"It will be good for his future because he will be able to move around easily and this will give him some independence."

This was the explanation during a long meeting at the Children's Institute conference room. They were trying to convince Soraya and me to accept a motorized wheelchair for Artur. When the salesperson was about to show us the wheelchairs in their catalogue, I asked to speak and my answer brought the room to an uncomfortable silence.

"I truly appreciate what this institution has been doing for my son and my family. With my poor vocabulary, I have no words to thank everybody. But I'd like you to donate this wheelchair to another child. I am confident that one day my son will walk on his own."

Taking this chair seemed like a life sentence for Artur, one that I was not about to accept, I thought.

The transplant team doctors decided it was time to close Artur's belly muscles, another major surgery. The physical therapist had been wondering if his big belly could be one of the factors that were interfering with his walking. We then decided to visit our reliable friend, Dr. Strauss. We wanted to get his advice regarding Artur's legs. Before our trip to Strasburg, Ellen Kaminski, Artur's outpatient physical therapist, encouraged us to discuss with Dr. Strauss the possibility of referring Artur to Shriner's Hospital of Philadelphia. She explained that this hospital does orthopedic surgery, mainly on kids, and it is a nonprofit organization.

After checking Artur's legs, Dr. Strauss agreed that we should take him to Shriner's Hospital.

"I'm glad that his therapist mentioned Shriner's. Their facility is great and they are able to perform a Gait Analysis that will determine exactly which muscles and nerves are keeping him from walking normally."

Dr. Strauss called a few days later and told us that the plan had changed. A branch of Shriner's Hospital in Erie, Pennsylvania, a city only two hours from Pittsburgh, would be more convenient for us. In the second half of 2007, we went to Shriner's in Erie where a team of highly skilled orthopedic professionals evaluated Artur. His examination was like something out of a science fiction movie and our king looked like a little astronaut. Fully clad in these special clothes and using a walker, he walked in the exam room, following a line marked on the floor. Special cameras filmed him and generated a three-dimensional computer image. We didn't understand much, but it was amazing to see his skeleton image on the monitor.

The examination took several hours, after which we were told that the tests would be analyzed and then the hospital would contact Dr. Strauss. A few days later, just as Dr. Strauss had predicted, Dr. James Sanders, the well-known orthopedic surgeon from Shriner's Hospital, said the lower muscles of Artur's legs were working against him.

As he had been proving during his whole life, Artur was born to be brave. In December 2007, at Children's Hospital of Pittsburgh, Artur underwent the surgery to reconnect his belly muscles and in January 2008, we went to Erie for his leg surgery. Artur was no longer a baby, at 6 years of age, he was aware of what was going on, so he was more scared about this second round of surgery. When he came back from the operating room with both legs in casts, Soraya had the tough task of calming him down and I had to console Vinicius. We were all in tears. On the second day, he was happy and enjoying the hospital's playroom.

When we returned to Pittsburgh, Artur's physical therapist, Ellen, was impressed with the results of his surgery. After several months as an inpatient, the CI decided to discharge him. When he came home, he was still walking with a walker or with crutches. With no difficulty, he was doing things that he couldn't have done before his leg surgeries. As an outpatient, our little king worked constantly on developing his walking skills. Besides the CI's therapy sessions, he also had some therapies at the Pioneer Elementary School, a public school located in the Brookline neighborhood, where Artur had been attending for a while. Pioneer had been recommended by the CI as one of the best schools in town for kids with special needs. Pioneer has a wonderful program, offering a great environment for learning as well as physical and occupational therapy. The staff was great; he loved his teacher, Carole Faloon, and his physical therapist.

The school and the CI coordinated their efforts, making us much more comfortable with Artur's post-surgical treatment. He was clearly becoming stronger; he never gave up on his exercises. Shortly thereafter, Ellen decided to try to let him walk using only one crutch. Her strategy was that using just one crutch would gently force him to improve his balance.

Artur was clearly working hard at it and we noticed that his balance, along with his confidence, seemed to be improving. Like all other children, Artur had lots of energy and he couldn't be quiet for a single minute. He had developed an unexplainable affinity for vacuum cleaners, and he would occasionally put his crutch aside and hold on to one of his Bissells while using it for balance.

In our Odyssey, another day to be remembered and celebrated was August 28, 2009. Artur was playing firefighter with Vinicius in the hallway. It was almost bedtime, so Soraya yelled to them.

"You guys, it's time to get ready for bed. Go to the bathroom and brush your teeth."

Soraya and I continued watching Law & Order. Vinicius came in quickly and headed for the bathroom. Minutes later, we sensed a shadow passing behind us. It couldn't be Vinicius; he had finished in the bathroom and was playing with his Legos right beside us. We turned to look, but couldn't believe it. Artur was walking toward the bathroom **on his own**, without his crutch!

At this, Soraya whispered to me before I could react.

"Shhhh! Let him go to the bathroom, and then let's see if he comes out without needing help."

And, **HE DID IT**! We heard the toilet being flushed, and then Artur walked out of the bathroom, staggering a little, but on his own two legs without any help. We couldn't contain our excitement. Artur was delighted with our excitement and Vinicius happily followed his brother all over the house. Artur did not care that we were crying. He could tell that we were happy and he began to show off by walking back and forth from his room to the hallway. Artur walked so much that evening that he got tired and fell asleep. This was, by far, the best day of our lives, something we had been praying for so long. There were times when we thought Artur would be wheelchair bound and never walk on his own. But, he never gave up and neither did we.

In the end, I was right in not accepting the motorized wheelchair.

My biggest fear was that he wouldn't be able to walk again in the morning.

Could this have been a one-time miracle?

When he got up, I was beside him. I gave him a hand as he headed for the bathroom. After a few steps, he released my hand and continued on his own.

On Saturday, the day after the real miracle, we were anxious for the coming week. We wanted to take him to his therapists at the Institute and teachers at Pioneer School. We were imagining how his therapist, Ellen, and the Children's Institute staff would react when they saw one of their **"Amazing Kids"** walking without his crutch.

When Monday came, we canceled his normal transport and drove him to school ourselves. When I took him out of his car seat, he escorted us directly to his classroom. His teacher, Carol Faloon, was the first one who noticed him walking on his own. In astonishment, she could only say.

"Oh, my God! Is that you?"

Tears started to flow. She reacted as if he were her son. She embraced him and gave him a big hug. She then called everybody to celebrate this victory. We thanked everyone there, certain that their efforts had been very important for Artur. Pioneer School had been and continues to be amazing to our son, and we are sure that everybody there loves him.

From Pioneer, we headed directly to the Institute. There, I found Ellen in the gym. I entered first, asking Soraya to hold Artur behind the door. I told Ellen that we had a surprise. Soraya then brought him into the gym. When Ellen saw him, she knelt down and burst into tears. Artur walked to her. She scooped him up, hugged him, and gave him a big kiss. She definitely needed some time to compose herself. With Artur like a trophy in her arms, she walked with us to show him to all of her colleagues. Christine and Denise were amazed. Enjoying the moment, Artur started showing off his walking, like he had at Pioneer. We thanked everybody and I told Ellen, in particular, that this couldn't have happened without her dedication and her belief that everything was possible.

This was truly a miracle, a real blessing. Words can't express our gratitude to God and to all the people who worked so hard for our beloved king.

CHAPTER 42

KING ARTUR

The best teacher that I ever had

When I look at my king, I cannot believe he is alive and healthy, a big boy. From the dark days starting shortly after his birth through his early childhood, until today, Artur's progress has been remarkable. Everything happened because of the miracle of modern science and especially because of the presence of God in our lives. Restoring my family life, I thank God every day for the angels and the good Samaritans. Especially, I thank Him for giving us the opportunity to have such a special child as Artur.

Early in his life, some people condemned Artur to life in a wheelchair, to being blind and deaf and even to die. Miraculously, my little King walks on his own, sees with a little help from his eyeglasses, and hears perfectly. Artur is bilingual. He reads and writes in English, speaks Portuguese fluently and is one of the best students in his class at Pioneer School. He still does physical therapy at the Children's Institute and has monthly appointments with the amazing transplant team at Children's Hospital of Pittsburgh to make sure that his new liver is working properly.

Every day, through his words and actions, Artur proves that he is doing great. God had prepared him to live. As bad as his journey was, now I am very comfortable with his life. It is good when it ends well, isn't it? Today, it is clear to me that the difficult road that my little king traveled had been paved before he was born, that God chose this path for him to teach us how to pursue happiness.

Why call the book *Sweet Odyssey*? Perhaps you have wondered this when reading about our bitter memories. How could such a journey be 'sweet'? Many people may have associated the title with the sweet smell that results from Maple Syrup Urine Disease, MSUD. Or perhaps, it is from the sweet fruits of Petrolina, the city where our King Artur was born. I chose this title for the sweetness of having children like Artur & Vinicius and a wife like Soraya. Having them in my life is part of an odyssey that I'll always do my best to make the sweetest possible.

From this sweet odyssey, I discovered that happiness is not a page on the social networks where everything is beautiful and people post just what they want; where life's problems are easily hidden and the world of fantasy sells us a false reality. Most often, we relate happiness with enjoyable moments, as when we take a vacation, or when we are doing well in life and when everything flows in our favor. I've learned and I can guarantee that this small and fleeting happiness has no roots. This kind of pleasure disappears as soon as we return to the routines and our day-to-day lives.

For me, happiness is achieved by understanding people and treating others the way I would treat myself and my family; by having the chance to kiss my wife and my kids every day; and by helping someone in need and doing it with love like so many have done for me and my family! Happiness results from constantly striving to improve as a human being. God put us in the world to evolve, and evolving our spirit is the only way we can achieve happiness.

Like God gave the anteater a long snout to feed himself and the chameleon the ability to change color to fend off predators, He gave us (human beings) our own characteristics and abilities that we often successfully hide from the world. With Artur, it was different. He accepted what God had planned for him and never gave up or complained about his mission.

Artur was engineered and polished by God to teach us how to love and to prove that nothing is impossible in the eyes of the Lord. Even in his worst days, he managed to comfort us with a smile.

Artur Bucar Santos - Always with a smile on his face

In December 2007, right after the surgery to close his belly muscles, almost two years after the transplant, we watched the Disney movie, *Madagascar*, in the recovery room. He had never seen it. He was quiet, but obviously in some pain when the movie character, "King Julian," danced into view and sang this song:

> "I like to move it, move it.
> She likes to move it, move it.
> He likes to move it, move it.
> You like to ("move it") …"

Just then, Artur started laughing and told me,

> "Dad, I like to move, too. But I don't know if I can, my belly hurts."

I didn't know what to say. I turned my face away from his and started crying. Smiling, he said, "Dad, put the music on again; this guy is crazy. Let's see it again."

Little did I know at that moment, but he was telling me that he was fine and I shouldn't be crying. He was telling me that a good laugh was going to heal him. He was telling me that he was OK. That night, he fell asleep to this movie, having played it at least three times. Like this, many were his lessons, not only for me, but also for everyone around him.

Every night before bed, I tell him that he is a special kid and I love him very much. I kiss his cheek and thank God for being blessed with this KING.

Among all the detours we faced during our odyssey, Artur never complained about anything. The happiest boy of all.

CHAPTER 43

THE FIGHT IS NOT OVER

The others are not only the others

To me, it is a miracle to be narrating this story. Today, Artur is cured; my family has been restored, and my children are living in a first-world country with many opportunities ahead. Not exactly how I had planned, but securing a future for my children and giving the comfort that my wife deserves was what I always wanted. This reminds me of part of a song written by a Brazilian musician, Leoni:

After you
The others are the others and that's it...

In other words, I could just move on with my new life and forget everything that happened. However, after what happened to my family, I wondered about the purpose of life. So, without a specific plan, but based on my promise to help other children in the same situation as my son, I proposed to divulge what I thought was needed by other families with MSUD kids, that is, INFORMATION - something that my family so clearly lacked early in our journey.

In January 2016, Arthur turned 14 years old. Since his birth, little has changed in Brazil to help children with metabolic disorders. Neonatal screening has not been expanded and many diseases including MSUD, Galactosemia, Humocistinuria, Tyrosinemia, Mucopolysaccharidosis, and many others, are still not being detected. The technology exists and just needs to be adopted. Only two laboratories in the entire country have the equipment capable of testing for amino acid levels that are so critical for kids with these disorders. Not only that, the tests take forever to process and to be reported. Consequently, Dr. Strauss and the Clinic for Special Children often performs these tests for Brazilian children. Brazilian families send their children's blood samples to the clinic in the USA, where Dr. Strauss runs the tests and prescribes a diet far faster than the Brazilian laboratories. Certainly, the Clinic for Special Children has been vital in helping children around the world. Desperate parents, often looking for help, request my support and, without hesitation, I ask my friend, Dr. Strauss, to help them. This amazing man has never refused to help.

Pioneering my cause gave me many scars, but it also gave me the honor of proving to those most incredulous that perseverance is a divine and powerful weapon. I had never imagined that my "ant work" would become a tool of hope for other families. But it has! Over the years, I've helped many children from Brazil, through my website (www.idariosantos.com) and my social network group (https://www.facebook.com/groups/136345209802112/). Some families have come to the United States to be treated and cured of their metabolic diseases.

I get calls, letters and emails from people struggling with similar problems. One day, Daniel Taissum called me from Rio de Janeiro, Brazil, telling me that his daughter, Leticia, had been diagnosed with MSUD. He had contacted Dr. Strauss and needed more information. "*You can ask anything you want*," I assured. A few months later, he came to our house and was startled by the amount of money he would have to spend. Dr. Strauss once again helped negotiate with the hospital and in a few months, Daniel and his family moved to Pittsburgh. Although I had requested him to never thank me, I received an email from Daniel, from which I memorized this passage:

"With each passing day that I have spent with the Santos family, they have shown me that the rough terrains are those that take us to the most beautiful places."

Perpetuating the chain of good will, I replied:

"I am glad to help you. In return, I only ask you do the same for other children who are in the same situation as your daughter."

This email encouraged me to create my new life challenge of helping other families who are dealing with children suffering from rare diseases.

My wish today is that "this chain of solidarity" will never stop growing and get my home country of Brazil and perhaps the world to treat children as they deserve. Here in the United States, the commitment to children varies from state to state, but all of them have laws that protect their children. In Brazil, things are quite different and I wondered, "What happens to a child born to a poor family, for example? What will happen if a baby is diagnosed with a metabolic disorder? How will the family be able to buy formula and seek proper treatment? Who will guide the treatment?" These questions torment me every day, and that's why I am committed to fight more and more for those families in need.

When the Brazilian court approved the financial support for Artur's case in 2005 to cover his treatment in the United States, the court ordered that Brazilian doctors be sent to the United States to be trained in the protocol. Back then, this had all been arranged with the American doctors at no charge. Unfortunately, Brazil has never sent a doctor to learn the protocol. With the right training, I know that Brazil could be doing it right.

Inspired and technically supported by Dr. Kevin Strauss and his team at the Clinic for Special Children (CSC), we are planning to establish a nonprofit organization to support children with Inborn Errors of Metabolism (IEM) in Brazil. A unit to screen and care for children with IEM, much like the CSC in the United States.

To mobilize our society and to promote the chance for a healthy life for those with rare diseases, I and my son Vinicius wrote a bill, the **Artur Bucar Santos Bill**, for presentation before the Brazilian congress. Artur's Law has the purpose of protecting children and adolescents in Brazil by giving them the basic right to early diagnosis, proper treatment and to ensure their right to life. This bill will guarantee that Brazil takes care of its greatest treasure - our children.

The Preliminary Provisions of Artur's Bill are:

TITLE I

PRELIMINARY DISPOSITIONS

Art. 1 – This Law creates mechanisms to guarantee the early diagnosis and treatment for children and adolescents suffering from Inborn Error of Metabolism – IEM, in accordance with §1 and §2, Art. 9 of the Children and Adolescents' Statute and Art. 6 of Brazil's Constitution. It also establishes measures to assist and protect families with children and adolescents suffering from IEM.

Art. 2 – Every child born in Brazil regardless of class, race, ethnicity, and sexual orientation of his/her parents, income, culture, educational level, and religion is entitled to enjoy fundamental human rights. The State shall ensure him/her the opportunity and means to live without any form of violence, to preserve his/her mental and physical well-being and provide resources for intellectual, social and moral development.

Art.3 – All Brazilian children born within national borders will be ensured all the necessary conditions for newborn screening for diseases related to IEM and will be allowed to exercise the rights to life, to safety, to health and to proper nourishment.

...

With all that said and with faith that people from my country, and especially the lawmakers, will embrace this noble cause, I declare that God has shown me a way of life. I can now revise Leoni's message and say "the others are NOT only the others and that WAS it." The many special kids should not be left to neglect. The Artur Bucar Santos Bill is the only way to give hope for those suffering from rare diseases. Fortunately, a federal congressman embraced our cause and presented our bill to the Brazilian House of Representatives. The bill #7374 is now being evaluated by a commission and hopefully will be voted on soon. I know we have a long way to go, but at least this is a beginning of a new era for our children.

CHAPTER 44

THE NEW BEGINNING

If you are in need, your old man will come through.

My dad, Hilario, encouraged me to write this book. He enjoys poetry, both reading it and writing it, so from time to time, he would comment that our odyssey sounded like a poem to be shared with the world. Now it is in your hands, and hopefully this book will inspire you to do good, because nothing will give you more pleasure than helping a child, especially a child with special needs.

I could call this chapter, "The End", but, in reality, I believe that everything is a new beginning. With hope, faith, pain, joy and happiness since the beginning of our journey, our lives have changed in so many ways. Had my wife's dreams been thwarted? How much did my son, Vinicius, suffer through this? What about my little king? How difficult was his struggle for survival? He had to eat a disgusting formula every day, have blood tests every week, he underwent multiple surgeries and go through therapy sessions every day, and still, he always had a smiling face. Indeed, my wife and kids were the real heroes. I always felt myself in a supporting role. Every night, I thank God for giving me a chance to have my family reunited

Recalling now our sweet 10-year odyssey, the major conclusion I can draw is that the wisdom of our elders can teach us a lot about living, but the strength of the young can impart an even greater source of life's inspiration. The greatest teacher in my life has been my little king, Artur. Through him, I have learned more about the purpose of life and about real love.

Today, I can say that I found my Grail, that my kingdom is in peace and that my children can dream about whatever they want. The "chest of our lives" as I referred in my introduction must be filled with people like Dr. Strauss and Dr. Pires and, therefore can become an important way of changing lives. Now, I feel that I should change my chest's name from the "chest of life" to the "chest of hope". HOPE for so many worldwide children suffering from lack of proper newborn screening and treatment. Together we can change the world's scenario. Let's give a chance to those neglected children and their families by giving them the ability to dream about their own kingdom.

The first step can be done by supporting institutions like the Clinic for Special Children. This is why I am donating 50% of my book royalties to the Clinic. In fact by reading this book you have already contributed to the meaningful work of the professional care givers at the Clinic for Special Children. However, you can do more! Simply ask your friends and family to buy *Sweet Odyssey* and/or donate money directly to the clinic: https://clinicforspecialchildren.org/give/. Your actions will help to provide children with a chance to live a healthy and happy life.

The next step is to ask our lawmakers to standardize newborn screening. For instance, here in the U.S. each state runs its own newborn screening program. Many states screen for a certain number of diseases, but some scan for more. Standardizing the screening program across the country will guarantee that all newborns have an equal chance of living a healthy life independent of where he/she is born.

In Brazil, as I mentioned earlier, the tests also vary from state to state and only a few disorders are screened. Diseases like MSUD are not detected in Brazil.

Some other countries do not even have a newborn screening program. AWARENESS and the implementation of sustainable newborn screening and treatment programs are the key to solving this problem. I finish this book with the amazing words of Dr. Holmes Morton founder of the Clinic for Special Children.

"Special children are not just interesting medical problems. Nor should they be called burdens to their families and communities. They are children who need our help. If we allow them to, they will teach us compassion. If we allow them to, they will teach us love. They will make us better scientists, better physicians, and more thoughtful people. - D. Holmes Morton"

God has given me the most amazing experience and the ability to understand what family really means.

Besides helping other children with IEM, I want this book to become a legacy for my own children, showing them that they have parents and an extended family that have fought hard for them and that we should never give up on our goals. Besides, helping people in need has been the most valuable lesson that I want to pass along to my children. I wonder, if we think to serve only ourselves, what would be the purpose of our lives?

- This is just priceless - Enjoying the spring time watching these amazing boys helping dad to take care of our lawn

POEM DEDICATED TO MY CHILDREN

Artur and Vinicius, this poem published by your grandpa's friend, inspired me to live focused on doing good and following the example of my parents. "Every time you want to remember me, read this poem as an example of my life."

ADVICE TO A GROWN UP SON
By: Sebastião Dias

My beloved son, please hear me well.

Your value in life, your Dad wants to tell.
Freedom is yours; you're almost an adult,
So, now as a man, you can walk as you will.

My duty to raise you has gone by the way,

But still, there are things that I need to say.
The future is yours; you now must decide.
God gave you life; now go seize the day.

Expect thorns at the start and hope for flowers at the end;
Respect others, do good, and never offend.
Wherever you go, stand firm in your place
So never will shame upon us descend.

Guard morality without bloodshed and help those in need.

And when you are needy, never risk a bad deed.

Stay close with your elders and care for kids,
Think of God, do your best, hard work is your creed.

Don't covet gold or love for a dream.
Choose a good woman to be on your team.
Do what I did, know how happy I am,
See your mother and I and our mutual esteem.

The world has two ways: the right and the wrong.
When choosing between them, you must always be strong.
But if you are facing a most difficult choice,
Follow me if you wish, my past is my song.

Even as you grow older, I'll be part of your endeavor
Teaching the best ways to face strife never.

Near or far, you will always be first on my mind;
I'm not just your dad, but your friend forever.

Travel the world and make friends as I knew.
Teach what I taught you; grow as I grew.
Enjoy your youth and seek honor and peace,
And if you're in need, your old man will come through.

THANKS

To name all the friends and health care providers who have helped us starting in Petrolina, passing through Fortaleza, Natal, Porto Alegre and ending here in the States would require me to write another book. However, some people were, and are, very special to our family. I apologize in advance for any omissions.

SPECIAL THANKS:

To my beloved and fantastic wife, Soraya; she always had a vision beyond the horizon.

       "Soraya - I love you so very much."

To our friend and superhero, Dr. Kevin Strauss

To Artur's godmother and our amazing friend, Camila Macedo

Dr. James Sanders & Shriner's Hospital of Erie

Ellen Kaminski; our physical therapist who never gave up on Artur;

The Stamps Family and their Foundation; their amazing work gave Artur a chance at a new life

Dr. Mazariegos and his transplant team at Children's Hospital of Pittsburgh;

Attorney Larry Lebowitz (Cohen&Grigsby). He inspired us to never give up.

To the Neumeyers (Lana & Fred). They are part our family.

To Bill Campbell (Artur's Godfather). Words will never be enough to describe how amazing he is. Bill, we love you.

To Ana Paula & Randy. They made our journey smoother

To my first and unforgettable friends in the United States, Bruno and Simone

To Joanne Kehris. You are very special.

To my American friends:

Eliezer and family, including the lovely Lilly Abreu;

Luiz Antonio and family; Viviane and Brent Rondon

To our super friend Leila Mandel and Moses Mandel

The amazing Dr. Mazariegos, the "Superman" Dr. Holmes Morton; doctors Kyle Soltys, Sindhi, James Bond; nurses Abigail, Shena, Kimberly, Alice, Tammy. The wonderful professionals at Children's Institute Tania, Stacey, Patsy, Christine, Denise and Patrick.

Dr. Diego Chaves, Annette Fiorenzo (special angels)

Thanks to Monica and Paulo Fontes; they always brought a lot of affection to our family;

Special thanks to all of you who are part of these wonderful institutions: The Clinic for Special Children, Children's Hospital of Pittsburgh, The Children's Institute, Amazing Kids, The Ronald McDonald House Charities, and Shriners Hospital of Erie

Our special thanks to Pioneer Education Center, especially to Carole Falone and Dr. Sylbia Kunst who welcomed our Artur with love. Thanks also to Sacred Heart Elementary School, especially Sister Lyn and Judy, who gave so much support to our Vinicius

Thanks to Ray and Angela who introduced us to the Brazilian community in Pittsburgh

To friends from Natal – RN, Brazil: Thanks to Glenia Fonseca, Tadeu Leal, Julia (Chico Carlo's sister), and the Fernandes Family. Dr. Bosco and Dr. Katia

To my friends from Fortaleza – CE, Brazil: My thanks to Archimedes Bucar, my brother-in-law and friend. To Sylvana Bucar, my sister-in-law; she was like a mother to our Artur. Many thanks to my mother-in-law, Gardenia Bucar, and my father-in-law, Archimedes Lages; they welcomed us for three long years, providing loving support for Soraya, Vinicius and Artur. Thanks to Jasmina, who got into my stories that amused Artur, and to Nadja Bortolotti.

My heartfelt thanks to all of my wife's relatives: Lysia, Antonio Filho and Ronaldo Bucar. Thanks to all of Soraya's aunts, uncles and cousins.

Thanks to the incredible grandma, Jasmina Waquim, and grandpa, Aruda Bucar; they always gave us support and love.

Thanks to Dr. Ivaldo Miranda, Dr. Ariosto Martins, Dr. Carla Soraya and Berlindes Bernardo. Thanks to the unforgettable Dr. Edda, Dr. Francielse, Dr. Izabella, Dr. Sonia, nurse Cacilda and to caregivers who, in one way or another, contributed to the welfare of our Artur.

Dr. Aluizio and Angela (Hospital Unimed Fortaleza)

To my friends from Petrolina: Special thanks to my brothers and sisters (Isnaldo, Ildeci, Irenice, Ildenice and Ivaldo); they never let me down. Thanks with love to my father, Hilario, and my mother, Beatriz; they have always been by my side from the beginning to end;

Thanks to Dr. Etelvina, Dr. Michele, Dr. Irene and all doctors and nurses from Memorial Hospital of Petrolina;

Thanks to my late grandfather, Sebastião. Even in the last days of his life, he never stopped asking about my children and Soraya.

And more thanks:

Edileusa Almeida, Stella Marcia and Sheila Mendes. Antonia (my sister's friend);

Thanks to Flavio and Airson Locio, Sealante and Saulo (great friends of my brother Isnaldo), the former mayor Fernando Bezerra Coelho, my friend Congressman Gonzaga Patriota, friends Danilo Savio, Graco Farias, Chico Carlos. Thanks to former congressman Oswaldo Coelho and family, Irene, Roberto Costa and family, Dr. Mello (attorney).

A portion of the proceeds from all sales benefits the Clinic for Special Children.

https://clinicforspecialchildren.org/give/

Made in the USA
Middletown, DE
13 May 2017